contents

easy comfort food

simple recipes for feel-good favourites

RYLAND PETERS & SMALL
LONDON • NEW YORK

Designers Iona Hoyle and Paul Stradling
Production Mai-Ling Collyer
Art Director Leslie Harrington
Editorial Director Julia Charles
Publisher Cindy Richards
Indexer Sandra Shotter

First published in 2008.
This updated edition published in 2018
by Ryland Peters & Small
20–21 Jockey's Fields
London WC1R 4BW
and
341 E 116th St
New York NY 10029
www.rylandpeters.com

10 9 8 7 6 5 4 3 2 1

Text © Fiona Beckett, Susannah Blake,
Tessa Bramley, Maxine Clark, Linda
Collister, Ross Dobson, Ursula Ferrigno,
Tonia George, Kate Habershon, Rachael
Anne Hill, Jennifer Joyce, Caroline
Marson, Jane Noraika, Louise Pickford,
Jennie Shapter, Sonia Stevenson, Fran
Warde, Laura Washburn and Ryland
Peters & Small 2008, 2018

Design and photographs
© Ryland Peters & Small 2008, 2018

ISBN 978-1-78879-042-0

Printed in China

A CIP record for this book is available
from the British Library.
US Library of Congress Cataloging-in-
Publication Data has been applied for.

Notes

• All spoon measurements are level unless otherwise specified.

• Both British (metric) and American (Imperial plus US cups) measurements are included in these recipes for your convenience; however it is important to work with one set of measurements and not alternate between the two within a recipe.

• All eggs are medium (UK) or large (US), unless specified as large, in which case US extra-large should be used. Uncooked or partly cooked eggs should not be served to the very young, the very old, those with compromised immune systems or to pregnant women.

• When a recipe calls for the grated zest of citrus fruit, buy unwaxed fruit and wash well before using. If you can only find treated fruit, scrub well in warm soapy water before using.

introduction

There is nothing more comforting than good, home-cooked food and it's easy to underestimate the uplifting effect that taking the time to cook delicious food can have. Here you'll find over 100 recipes to satisfy every craving and mood. Whether you are in need of a hearty, satisfying meal on a cold winter's day or a sweet indulgence to help chase away the blues, you're guaranteed to find just the recipe you need here.

Soups & Savoury Snacks is full of quick-fix comfort classics. Lift your spirits with a steaming bowl of soup or something warm and toasted, oozing with melted cheese. Week-day dining dilemmas are also solved in Supper Dishes, where you'll find lots of indulgent yet simple ideas, perfect for welcoming your loved ones home after a tough day at work or school. Feeding the family can be a challenge, but Bakes, Casseroles & Roasts offers plenty of great solutions. What could be more inviting than a freshly baked pie or a roast with all the trimmings? Cakes & Teatime Treats will always be a hit with adults and kids alike, so why not bake up a batch of brownies or cupcakes? Last but not least, delicious cold and hot Desserts cannot fail to improve even the dreariest of days!

soups &
savoury snacks

Synonymous with bistro eating, and often served at French weddings in the early hours after a long night of celebrating. This simplified version is ideal when it's chilly and there are only a few onions lurking about.

french onion soup

50 g/3 tablespoons unsalted butter

1 tablespoon extra virgin olive oil

3 large onions, about 1.3 kg/3 lbs., thinly sliced

2 garlic cloves, crushed

1 tablespoon plain/all-purpose flour

1 litre/4 cups beef or chicken stock

600 ml/2¾ cups dry white wine

1 fresh bay leaf

2 sprigs of thyme

1 baguette, or other white bread, sliced

about 180 g/1½ cups freshly grated Gruyère cheese

coarse salt and freshly ground black pepper

serves 4–6

Put the butter and oil in a large saucepan and melt over medium heat. Add the onions and cook over low heat until soft, 15–20 minutes.

Add the garlic and flour and cook, stirring, for about 1 minute. Add the stock, wine, bay leaf and thyme. Season with salt and pepper and bring to the boil. Boil for 1 minute, then lower the heat and simmer very gently for 20 minutes. Taste and adjust the seasoning with salt and pepper. At this point, the soup will be cooked, but standing time will improve the flavour – at least 30 minutes.

Before serving, preheat the grill/broiler. Put the baguette slices on a baking sheet and brown under the grill/broiler until lightly toasted. Set aside.

To serve, ladle the soup into ovenproof bowls and top with a few toasted baguette rounds. Sprinkle grated cheese over the top and cook under the grill/broiler until browned and bubbling. Serve immediately.

The trick to making rich stock is to brown the chicken first and cover while simmering. The result is a flavoursome base which suits any additions. These noodles are classic, but you can try rice or matzo balls.

chicken noodle soup

2 tablespoons olive oil

1.4 kg/3 lbs. chicken drumsticks and thighs

1 onion, chopped

1 carrot, chopped

1 garlic clove, sliced

2 celery ribs/stalks, chopped

1 bouquet garni (bay leaf, thyme and parsley)

to finish

1 onion, chopped

2 large carrots, sliced 1 cm/½ inch thick

2 celery ribs/stalks, sliced 2 cm/1 inch thick

90 g/3 oz. fine egg noodles, broken into pieces

20 g/¼ cup fresh flat leaf parsley, finely chopped

sea salt and freshly ground black pepper

serves 4

Heat 1 tablespoon of the olive oil in a large, heavy stockpot. Season the chicken pieces and brown them in the pot in batches. Put all the chicken pieces back in the pot with the onion, carrot, garlic and celery, and cook over low heat for 15 minutes. Pour in 1.5 litres/6 cups water, add the bouquet garni and simmer, covered, for 1 hour over medium/low heat. Remove any foamy scum from the surface during cooking.

Strain the finished stock through a fine sieve into a bowl and skim off any excess fat. Reserve the chicken and leave to cool before removing the meat from the bones and roughly chopping it.

To finish, heat the remaining olive oil in a saucepan. Add the onion, carrots and celery, and season. Sauté for 5 minutes, then pour in the stock. Bring to the boil and add the noodles. Cook until the noodles are al dente, then add the chopped chicken. Sprinkle in the chopped parsley, stir and serve.

Once everything is peeled and chopped, this country-style chunky soup is surprisingly simple to make. The roasted vegetables have a sweet but intense flavour. For a smoother texture, push through a sieve when cooked.

roasted vegetable soup

700 g/2 lbs. ripe plum tomatoes, halved

1 red onion, finely chopped

2 carrots, finely chopped

1 small red chilli/chile, left whole

2 garlic cloves, peeled but left whole

a few fresh thyme or rosemary sprigs

2 tablespoons olive oil

350 ml/1⅓ cups passata/ sieved tomatoes

½ teaspoon sugar

a squeeze of fresh lime juice

sea salt and freshly ground black pepper

a handful of fresh coriander/cilantro, roughly chopped

a drizzle of extra virgin olive oil and warm crusty bread, to serve

serves 2–4

Preheat the oven to 200°C (400°F) Gas 6.

Put the plum tomatoes, onions and carrots in a roasting pan. Add the chilli/chile, garlic, thyme or rosemary sprigs and olive oil and toss until the vegetables are well coated in the oil. Place in the preheated oven and roast for about 25 minutes, turning the vegetables occasionally using a large spoon.

Remove from the oven and discard the chilli/chile. Blend the roasted vegetables, garlic and herbs with the passata/sieved tomatoes to the desired consistency in a blender or food processor or using a hand-held blender. Add the sugar, lime juice and 150 ml/⅔ cup cold water, and season well with salt and pepper.

Pour the mixture into a large pan and gently heat through. Add the chopped coriander/cilantro just before serving. Ladle into warmed serving bowls and drizzle with a little extra virgin olive oil. Serve immediately with warm crusty bread.

Try to find a small, creamy-white, whole head of cauliflower for this deliciously cheesy soup. Instead of Gruyère, you could add the same quantity of a sharp, aged Cheddar for a 'cauliflower gratin'-flavour.

creamy cauliflower & gruyère soup

2 tablespoons butter

1 onion, roughly chopped

1 celery rib/stalk, chopped

1 small cauliflower, about 1 kg/2 lbs., cut into small pieces

1.5 litres/6 cups vegetable or chicken stock

250 ml/1 cup double/heavy cream

200 g/2 cups Gruyère cheese, grated, plus extra to serve

sea salt and freshly ground black pepper

freshly chopped parsley and toasted wholemeal/whole-wheat bread, to serve

serves 4

Heat the butter in a saucepan over high heat. Add the onion and celery and cook for 5 minutes, until the onion has softened but not browned.

Add the cauliflower pieces and stock and bring to the boil. Allow to boil for 25–30 minutes, until the cauliflower is really soft and breaking up in the stock.

Transfer the mixture to a food processor or blender and process the mixture in batches until smooth. Return the purée to a clean saucepan. Add the cream and cheese and cook over low heat, stirring constantly, until the cheese has all smoothly melted into the soup.

Season to taste with a little salt and black pepper. Serve sprinkled with chopped parsley and extra cheese and with hot buttered wholemeal/whole-wheat toast on the side.

From the land of haggis, kippers, neeps and tatties comes a dead-simple version of its famous namesake broth. Instead of traditional barley, brown rice is used here. Add some thyme if you like herbs.

scotch broth

2 tablespoons light olive oil

1 carrot, diced

1 leek, diced

2 celery ribs/stalks, diced and leaves chopped

500 g/1 lb. stewing lamb, well trimmed of fat and cubed

500 ml/2 cups chicken stock

1 tablespoon light soy sauce

95 g/½ cup brown rice

sea salt and freshly ground black pepper

4 soft dinner rolls, buttered, to serve

serves 4

Heat the oil in a large saucepan. Add the carrot, leek, celery ribs/stalks and leaves and cook over high heat for 5 minutes, stirring often. Add the lamb, stock, soy sauce, rice and 1 litre/4 cups water and bring to the boil.

Reduce the heat to low, cover with a tight-fitting lid and leave the soup to simmer for 1 hour. Season to taste with salt and black pepper and serve with the soft, buttered rolls on the side.

Puy lentils, grown in France, are great at thickening soups without turning sludgy. They give this soup a little bite which is offset by the soft, buttery vegetables and enriched by the heady tang of the dried oregano.

chunky puy lentil & vegetable soup

50 g/3 tablespoons butter

2 carrots, finely chopped

2 leeks, white part only, thinly sliced

1 large onion, finely chopped

3 garlic cloves, sliced

½ teaspoon dried chilli/ red pepper flakes

2 teaspoons dried oregano

a 400-g/14-oz. can chopped plum tomatoes

200 g/1 cup small green lentils, preferably Puy lentils

1 litre/4 cups vegetable stock

sea salt and freshly ground black pepper

crusty bread, toasted and buttered, and freshly grated pecorino or Parmesan cheese, to serve

serves 4–6

Melt the butter in a large casserole dish or heavy-based saucepan. Add the carrots, leeks, onion and garlic and a large pinch of salt. Stir until everything is coated in butter and cook over medium heat, with the lid on, for 15 minutes, stirring occasionally.

Once the vegetables have softened, add the chilli/red pepper flakes, oregano, tomatoes, lentils and stock. Cover again and leave to simmer for 30 minutes, or until the lentils are cooked. Season with salt and freshly ground pepper to taste.

Transfer to bowls and serve with buttered toast and grated pecorino or Parmesan cheese on the side.

This recipe is based on a delicious soup from Tom's Kitchen, restaurants founded by top London chef Tom Aikens. His version had chicken stock, which you could use too, but the version here is vegetarian.

pumpkin soup with honey & sage

75 g/5 tablespoons unsalted butter

1 small to medium onion, roughly chopped

1 carrot, finely chopped

1 garlic clove, peeled and crushed

1 kg/2¼ lbs. pumpkin or butternut squash, seeded, peeled and cubed

2 heaped tablespoons clear honey

3 sprigs of sage

750 ml/3 cups vegetable stock made with an organic vegetable stock cube or 1 level tablespoon vegetable bouillon powder

75 ml/⅓ cup double/heavy cream

lemon juice, salt and freshly ground black pepper to taste

crisp-fried sage leaves and crusty bread, to serve

serves 4–6

Gently melt the butter in a large lidded saucepan or casserole. Add the onion and carrot, stir, cover and cook over low heat for about 4–5 minutes. Add the cubed pumpkin or squash, honey and sage, stir, replace the lid and continue to cook very gently for about 10 minutes.

Pour in the stock, bring to the boil and cook for about 10 minutes until the vegetables are soft. Turn off the heat and leave the soup to cool slightly, then remove the sage and sieve the soup, reserving the liquid.

Put half the cooked vegetables into a blender or food processor with just enough of the reserved cooking liquid to blend into a smooth purée. Transfer to a clean pan and repeat with the remaining vegetables, adding the purée to the first batch. Whizz the remaining liquid in the blender or food processor to pick up the last bits of purée and add that too. Bring the soup slowly to the boil, then stir in the cream without boiling further.

Season to taste with about 1 tablespoon of lemon juice and 1 teaspoon of salt, and black pepper. Serve with an extra swirl of cream or scatter some crisp-fried sage leaves on top and serve with crusty wholewheat or multi-grain bread.

Inspired by the classic Welsh rarebit, this substantial snack will keep hunger pangs at bay. Enjoy big, manly slabs of toast, or cut the bread into delicate fingers before toasting and topping with the cheese mixture.

melting cheese & sun-dried tomatoes on toast

1 tablespoon olive oil

1 shallot, finely chopped

2 tablespoons white wine

50 g/½ cup grated Cheddar or similar sharp cheese

½ teaspoon cornflour/cornstarch, mixed with 1 teaspoon water

2 thick slices of white bread

½ garlic clove

2 sun-dried tomatoes in olive oil, cut into thin strips

2 sprigs of fresh oregano

dried chilli/red pepper flakes, for sprinkling

serves 1

Heat the oil in a small pan and add the shallot. Sauté gently for about 5 minutes until translucent. Stir in the wine and cheese, then the cornflour/cornstarch mixture. Heat gently, stirring, until the cheese has melted and the mixture is creamy.

Meanwhile, toast the bread on one side. Turn it over, rub with the cut side of the garlic, pour over the cheese and grill/broil until golden and bubbling. Remove from the heat and top with the strips of sun-dried tomato, oregano and a sprinkling of dried chilli/red pepper flakes.

Another treat that's good anytime, these juicy mushrooms are rich and garlicky. Pile them on thick slices of hot buttered toast or crusty bread; if you're feeling indulgent, add a spoonful of mascarpone.

mushrooms on toast

1 tablespoon olive oil

2 shallots, finely sliced

1 garlic clove, finely chopped

150 g/6 oz. button mushrooms

60 ml/¼ cup white wine

1 sprig of thyme, plus extra to serve (optional)

2 thick slices of wholemeal/ whole-wheat bread or country-style sourdough

butter, for spreading

sea salt and freshly ground black pepper

serves 2

Heat the oil in a pan, add the shallots and fry gently for 2 minutes, then add the garlic and cook for a further minute.

Add the mushrooms, toss to coat in the garlicky oil, then add the white wine, thyme and a pinch of salt. Increase the heat and bring to the boil, then bubble gently for about 10 minutes until the mushrooms are tender and the juices have been absorbed.

When the mushrooms are nearly cooked, toast the bread on both sides and spread with the butter. Season the mushrooms with pepper, check if they need any more salt, then pile onto the toast. Top with fresh thyme, if using, and serve.

This manly feast is perfect after a late night out. The potatoes absorb the chorizo flavours, and the spicy, garlicky oil soaks deliciously into the toast. For even more heat, sprinkle with extra chilli/red pepper flakes.

spicy fried potatoes & chorizo on toast

3 tablespoons olive oil

200 g/6 oz. new potatoes, boiled and cut into bite-sized chunks

125 g/4 oz. chorizo sausage, cut into bite-sized chunks

1 garlic clove, crushed

½ teaspoon crushed dried chillies/ red pepper flakes

4 slices of country-style sourdough bread

sea salt and freshly ground black pepper

serves 2

Heat the oil in a large frying pan/skillet until hot, then add the potatoes and fry for about 5 minutes. Add the chorizo and continue frying, turning occasionally, until the potatoes are crisp and golden. Sprinkle with the garlic and dried chillies/red pepper flakes and fry for a further 2 minutes.

Meanwhile, toast the bread on both sides. Spoon the potato and chorizo mixture on top, drizzling over any extra oil from the pan, then serve.

The very best tuna melts are always towering, melting extravaganzas. Use any white bread — crusty rustic sourdough, a large bloomer, a freshly baked sandwich loaf — just make sure the slices are large and thick.

tuna melt

200 g/6 oz. canned tuna, drained

3–3½ tablespoons mayonnaise

½ tablespoon capers, rinsed and finely chopped

2 cornichons/gherkins or 1 large dill pickle in sweet vinegar, diced fairly finely, plus extra to serve

¼ red (bell) pepper, diced fairly finely

1 tablespoon chopped fresh tarragon

2 large, thick slices of white crusty bread

4 large, thin slices of Swiss cheese, such as Gruyère or Emmenthal

freshly ground black pepper

serves 2

Put the tuna in a bowl and flake the flesh. Add the mayonnaise, capers, cornichons/gherkins, (bell) peppers and tarragon and mix well. Season with plenty of black pepper.

Toast the bread on one side under a preheated grill/broiler, then turn it over and spread the tuna thickly on the uncooked side. Put 2 cheese slices on top of each toast and grill/broil for about 5 minutes until the cheese is golden and bubbling. Serve with extra pickles.

Note Look for tuna canned in water rather than brine — the capers are salty enough already.

There is something wonderful about using leftovers. Save your leftover baked or roasted potatoes to create this satisfying breakfast panino, which is worth cooking extra potatoes for in the first place.

bacon, potato & red leicester panini with tabasco sauce

1 ciabatta loaf

6 slices of smoked bacon

1 large cooked potato, sliced

2 teaspoons Tabasco sauce

50 g/2 oz. Red Leicester or Monterey Jack cheese, thinly sliced

sea salt and freshly ground black pepper

vegetable oil, for frying and brushing

panini press

makes 2 panini

Preheat a panini press. Cut the top and bottom off the ciabatta so that it is about 3 cm/1¼ inches thick. Save the crusts for another use. Slice open lengthways and then cut in half.

Add a little oil to a frying pan/skillet and fry the bacon until crisp. Remove from the pan and drain on paper towels. Keep the pan hot, add the potato slices and season with salt and pepper. Fry on both sides until crisp around the edges. Divide the bacon and potatoes between the two sandwiches. Add a dash of Tabasco and top with cheese. Brush both sides of the panini with a little oil and toast in the preheated panini press for 3 minutes, or according to the manufacturer's instructions. The bread should be golden brown and the filling warmed through.

Large flour tortillas make perfect wraps — these are filled with that perennially perfect combination of bacon, lettuce and tomato, and then cooked on a stove-top grill pan for a yummy toasted sandwich.

blt tortilla panini

16 slices of smoked pancetta
or bacon

4 large flour tortillas

4 ripe tomatoes, sliced

125 g/4 oz. Gruyère cheese, sliced

125 g/2 cups crisp lettuce,
shredded

4 tablespoons mayonnaise

salt and freshly ground
black pepper

serves 4

Put the pancetta or bacon slices in a dry frying pan/skillet over medium heat and cook gently until golden and crispy.

Put the tortillas on a work surface and arrange 4 bacon slices down the centre of each one. Top with the tomatoes, cheese, lettuce and mayonnaise, lightly sprinkling with salt and pepper as you go.

Fold the edges over to form a wrap and cook seam side down in a hot stove-top grill pan for 2 minutes. Flip and cook for a further 2 minutes on the second side. Serve hot.

If you like cheese, then cheese-on-toast is always a winner. This simple combination gives the classic an extra dimension and tastes like heaven. Make sure that you squeeze the grated courgette/zucchini well.

courgettes & cheddar on toast

2 courgettes/zucchini, grated

200 g/1²/₃ cups mature/sharp Cheddar cheese, grated

1 shallot, finely diced

1 small egg

a dash of Worcestershire sauce

4 slices of bread, toasted

sea salt and freshly ground black pepper

serves 4

Put the grated courgettes/zucchini in a kitchen cloth and twist tightly, squeezing out all the excess liquid.

Transfer to a mixing bowl and add the cheese, shallot, egg, a dash of Worcestershire sauce, salt and pepper. Stir thoroughly.

Put the toasted bread onto a baking sheet, pile the courgette/zucchini mixture on top and cook under a preheated grill/broiler until golden brown. Serve hot.

Children love French toast, also sometimes called eggy bread. Top it with fried tomatoes to make a juicy, tasty snack fit for all ages. Frying tomatoes intensifies their flavour and the heat makes them soft and velvety.

french toast & fried tomatoes

4 eggs

4 tablespoons milk

4 slices of bread

50 g/4 tablespoons butter

4 ripe or green tomatoes, halved

sea salt and freshly ground black pepper

serves 4

Beat together the eggs, milk and some salt and pepper in a large, shallow dish. Add the bread and leave to soak for 5 minutes on each side so that all the egg mixture is absorbed.

Heat a large, non-stick frying pan/skillet over medium heat. Add the soaked bread and cook over medium/low heat for 3–4 minutes on each side.

In a separate frying pan/skillet, melt the butter. Add the tomatoes and fry on each side for 2 minutes, then serve on top of the hot French toast.

This recipe is based on a favourite Greek dish —
gigantes, which roughly translates as 'big beans'. Make
the Tomato Sauce, a very versatile recipe which can
be added to enliven many different dishes, ahead.

home-made baked beans

2 tablespoons extra virgin olive oil

1 onion, chopped

½ teaspoon dried chilli/
red pepper flakes

800 g/1¾ cups canned butter/lima
beans, rinsed and drained

1 recipe Tomato Sauce (page 68)

sea salt and freshly ground
black pepper

toast and freshly grated Parmesan
cheese, to serve

serves 4

Heat the oil in a saucepan and gently fry the onion and chilli/hot red pepper flakes for 10 minutes until softened but not golden.

Add the beans, stir once and then add the tomato sauce. Bring to the boil, cover with a lid and simmer gently for about 20 minutes. Taste and adjust the seasoning with salt and pepper and serve piled onto toast with a sprinkling of freshly grated Parmesan.

Toasted cheese made with lurid orange cheese is surely a fond memory of most childhoods. This grown-up version made with real cheese is even better, and is delicious served with Bread-and-Butter Pickles.

grilled ham & cheese sandwiches with pickle

4 thick slices of mature Cheddar or Gruyère cheese

8 pieces of sourdough bread, sliced 1 cm/½ inch thick

2 teaspoons Worcestershire sauce

4 slices of good-quality ham

4 tablespoons butter

sea salt and freshly ground pepper

bread-and-butter pickles

500 g/1 lb. Lebanese/Kirby cucumbers

2 small onions, cut into thick rings

300 ml/1¼ cups cider vinegar

300 g/2 cups sugar

1 tablespoon salt

1 tablespoon yellow mustard seeds

1 teaspoon celery seeds

3 sprigs of fresh dill

1 teaspoon black peppercorns

crisps/potato chips and mustard, to serve

serves 4

To make the bread-and-butter pickles, slice the cucumbers 1 cm/½ inch thick with a corrugated vegetable slicer or a normal knife. In a medium bowl, soak the onions and cucumber slices in ice water for 1 hour. Place all the remaining ingredients in a medium saucepan with 150 ml/²⁄₃ cup water and bring to the boil. Drain the cucumber and onions and put them in a large glass jar or sealable container. Pour the hot liquid over and leave to cool slightly before refrigerating. Chill for 24 hours before eating. Use within 1 week.

When you are ready to make the sandwiches, place the slices of Cheddar on 4 pieces of the bread. Sprinkle each with ½ teaspoon Worcestershire sauce and top with a slice of ham. Cover each with a slice of bread. Spread 1 tablespoon of the butter on the outside of each sandwich. Give each a sprinkle of salt and pepper.

Heat a large, heavy, non-stick frying pan/skillet. If you have only a small pan, make the sandwiches in batches. Put them in the frying pan/skillet over medium/low heat for about 3–4 minutes on each side, or until brown. Cut each sandwich in half diagonally and serve while warm. Serve with the bread-and-butter pickles, crisps/potato chips and your favourite mustard to dip in.

There are two ways of cooking scrambled eggs: in the microwave or on the stovetop in a non-stick pan. The second method allows you to stir the eggs, resulting in truly creamy perfection.

scrambled eggs

6 eggs

4 tablespoons milk

30 g/2 tablespoons butter

sea salt and freshly ground black pepper

snipped fresh chives, to serve

serves 2–3

Whisk the eggs together with the milk and seasoning.

Melt the butter in a non-stick pan, then add the egg mixture, stirring frequently until it reaches a creamy consistency. Serve with a sprinkling of chopped chives and hot buttered toast. For a real treat, you can add a few slices of smoked salmon.

Fry the Parma ham until really crisp, if you want to add a lovely texture to the creamy sauce and egg yolks. Substitute smoked salmon for the ham or, for a meat-free version, replace the ham with wilted spinach.

eggs benedict

4 large slices of Parma ham/prosciutto

4 eggs

1 tablespoon vinegar, preferably distilled

4 plain English muffins

hollandaise sauce

250 g/2 sticks unsalted butter

3 egg yolks

2 tablespoons water

1 teaspoon freshly squeezed lemon juice

sea salt and freshly ground black pepper

serves 4

To make the hollandaise sauce, put the butter in a small saucepan and melt gently over very low heat, without letting it brown. Put the egg yolks, water and lemon juice into a blender and process until frothy. With the blade turning, gradually pour in the melted butter in a steady stream until the sauce is thickened and glossy. Transfer the sauce to a bowl set over a saucepan of hot water. Cover and keep the sauce warm.

Grill/broil or fry the slices of ham until really crisp and keep them warm in a low oven.

To poach the eggs, bring a saucepan of lightly salted water to the boil. Add the vinegar and reduce to a gentle simmer. Swirl the water well with a fork and crack 2 eggs into the water. Cook for 3 minutes, remove with a slotted spoon and repeat with the remaining 2 eggs.

Meanwhile, toast the muffins whole and top each with a slice of crispy ham. Put the poached eggs on top of the ham. Spoon over the hollandaise, sprinkle with salt and pepper and serve at once.

Note To poach eggs in advance, follow the directions above and as soon as the eggs are cooked, plunge them into iced water. Just before serving, return them to a saucepan of gently boiling water for a few seconds to heat through.

This is a great way to cook an omelette – once prepared, it can finish cooking in the oven, making the whole thing quite relaxed for a late, lazy breakfast. Make sure the pan handle is ovenproof or removable.

baked brunch omelette

2 tablespoons sunflower oil

4 slices of smoked bacon, cut into strips

1 onion, thinly sliced

1 potato, cubed

75 g/3½ oz. button mushrooms, sliced

5 large eggs

90 ml/scant ½ cup milk

75 g/¾ cup grated mature Cheddar/ sharp cheese

1 tablespoon unsalted butter

1 tablespoon freshly grated Parmesan cheese

sea salt and freshly ground black pepper

20-cm/8-inch ovenproof non-stick frying pan/skillet (measure the base, not the top)

serves 2–3

Preheat the oven to 200°C (400°F) Gas 6.

Heat the oil in the frying pan/skillet, add the bacon, onion and potato and fry for 6 minutes, or until the potatoes start to brown. Add the mushrooms and fry for 2 minutes.

Meanwhile put the eggs and milk in a large bowl and whisk briefly with a fork, just enough to mix the yolks and whites. Season with salt and plenty of pepper. Stir in three-quarters of the Cheddar.

Using a slotted spoon, transfer the potato mixture to the bowl of eggs and mix well. Add the butter to the frying pan/skillet and, when it starts to foam, pour in the omelette mixture. Sprinkle with the remaining cheese and transfer to the preheated oven.

Cook for 12–15 minutes, or until just set. Loosen the edges with a spatula or palette knife and slide onto a warmed serving plate. Sprinkle with Parmesan and serve immediately.

Originally served in American diners, along with favourites like Denver omelette, *huevos rancheros* has become justifiably popular. You can use storebought salsa for this but make sure it is the cooked variety.

huevos rancheros

4 corn tortillas

3 tablespoons pure vegetable oil

60 g/1 cup grated mild Cheddar cheese

4 eggs

sea salt and freshly ground black pepper

salsa

6 plum tomatoes, halved

2 jalapeño peppers

8 garlic cloves, unpeeled

4 tablespoons/¼ cup chopped fresh coriander/cilantro

1 teaspoon Tabasco Sauce or other favourite hot sauce

1 small red onion, finely chopped, to serve

serves 4

To make the salsa, place the halved tomatoes cut side up in a shallow roasting pan. Season and place on the top rack under a preheated grill/broiler. Grill/broil for about 10 minutes, or until charred.

In a dry, non-stick frying pan/skillet, char the peppers and garlic cloves. Keep turning to colour all sides. When done, peel the garlic and place in a food processor. Put the peppers in a plastic bag, tie a knot in the bag and leave the peppers to steam for a few minutes, then peel, seed and stem. Add the flesh to the food processor along with the tomatoes, 2 tablespoons of the coriander/cilantro and the Tabasco. Season and pulse until smooth. Pour into a saucepan and cook briefly over medium heat to warm through.

Preheat the oven to 200°C (400°F) Gas 6.

Brush the tortillas with 2 tablespoons of the oil and bake for 5 minutes until golden. Divide the cheese between the tortillas and return to the oven for 5 minutes until the cheese has melted. Turn off the oven, open the door and leave the tortillas in to keep warm. Fry the eggs in a non-stick frying pan/skillet in the remaining tablespoon of oil. Place the tortillas on 4 plates and slip an egg on top of each. Spoon the warm salsa over each and sprinkle with the chopped onion and remaining coriander/cilantro.

The British invented bubble and squeak to use up leftovers from a dinner of beef brisket, potato and cabbage. Americans dropped the cabbage and called it corned beef hash — a hearty savoury breakfast dish.

corned beef hash

3 baking potatoes (700 g/1½ lbs.), peeled and diced

3 tablespoons butter

1 onion, diced

1 garlic clove, finely chopped

300 g/10 oz. cooked corned beef brisket, diced

½ teaspoon Tabasco Sauce

1 tablespoon pure vegetable oil

4 eggs

serves 4

Boil the potatoes in salted water for about 6 minutes, then drain and put in a large bowl. Heat 1 tablespoon of the butter in a large, heavy frying pan/skillet. Add the onion, garlic and corned beef. Season and sauté for 5 minutes. Pour the mixture into the bowl with the potatoes. Add the Tabasco and mix well.

Add the remaining butter to the frying pan/skillet. Pour the potato mixture into it and press everything down firmly. Cover with a heavy lid or plate that will fit just inside the pan to weight the mixture down. Cook over medium heat for 10 minutes. Turn the mixture over in batches and cook for 10 minutes on the other side. The meat should be brown and crisp; keep cooking and turning if it isn't.

Make 4 indentations in the potatoes and crack an egg into each. Place a fitted lid over the pan and cook until the eggs are done. Alternatively, in a separate non-stick frying pan/skillet, heat 1 tablespoon vegetable oil and fry the eggs. Place one fried egg on top of each serving of corned beef hash. You can also poach the eggs instead of frying them.

supper dishes

Fontina, Gorgonzola, Taleggio and Parmesan are four favourite Italian cheeses. Mix and match your own selection, choosing ones that are creamy with a good flavour. Use at room temperature for maximum taste.

four cheeses risotto

900 ml/4 cups vegetable stock

50 g/4 tablespoons unsalted butter

1 tablespoon olive oil

8 shallots, finely chopped

1 garlic clove, crushed

275 g/1½ cups risotto rice, such as vialone nano, carnaroli or arborio

about 125 ml/½ cup white wine

100 g/1½ cups freshly grated Parmesan cheese, plus extra to serve

50 g/2 oz. Gorgonzola cheese, cut into cubes

50 g/2 oz. Fontina cheese, cut into cubes

50 g/2 oz. Taleggio cheese, rind removed and cheese cut into cubes

a handful of fresh flat leaf parsley, coarsely chopped

sea salt and freshly ground black pepper

serves 4

Put the stock in a saucepan. Heat until almost boiling, then reduce the heat until barely simmering to keep it hot.

Heat the butter and oil in a sauté pan or heavy-based casserole over medium heat. Add the shallots and cook for 1–2 minutes, until softened but not browned. Add the garlic and mix well.

Add the rice and stir, using a wooden spoon, until the grains are well coated and glistening, about 1 minute. Pour in the wine and stir until it has been completely absorbed.

Add 1 ladle of hot stock and simmer, stirring until it has been absorbed. Continue to add the stock at intervals and cook as before, until the liquid has been absorbed and the rice is tender but still firm (al dente), about 18–20 minutes. Reserve the last ladle of stock.

Add the reserved stock, the four cheeses, parsley, salt and pepper. Mix well. Remove from the heat, cover and leave to rest for 2 minutes.

Spoon into warmed bowls, sprinkle with grated Parmesan and serve.

This is traditional Italian food, but with a pleasing modern twist. Substantial as well as comforting, the recipe for this rich, creamy risotto is derived from a dish served at Peck — a wonderful restaurant in Milan.

mushroom, cognac & cream risotto

100 g/½ cup unsalted butter

275 g/8 oz. large, open-cap mushrooms, finely sliced

1 tablespoon Cognac or other brandy

3 tablespoons single/light cream

900 ml/4 cups vegetable stock

1 tablespoon olive oil

8 shallots, finely chopped

2 garlic cloves, crushed

275 g/1½ cups risotto rice, such as vialone nano, carnaroli or arborio

100 g/1½ cups freshly grated Parmesan cheese, plus shavings to serve

a handful of fresh flat leaf parsley, coarsely chopped

sea salt and freshly ground black pepper

serves 4

Heat half the butter in a frying pan/skillet until foaming, then add the mushrooms and cook for 5 minutes. Add salt and pepper. Add the Cognac or brandy, boil until reduced by half, then stir in the cream. Simmer for 5 minutes, until the sauce has thickened slightly. Set aside.

Put the stock in a saucepan. Heat until almost boiling, then reduce the heat until barely simmering to keep it hot.

Heat the remaining butter and oil in a sauté pan or heavy-based casserole over medium heat. Add the shallots and cook for 1–2 minutes, until softened but not browned. Add the garlic and rice and stir, using a wooden spoon, until the grains are well coated and glistening, about 1 minute.

Add 1 ladle of hot stock and simmer, stirring until it has been absorbed. Continue to add the stock at intervals and cook as before, until the liquid has been absorbed and the rice is tender but firm (al dente), about 18–20 minutes.

Add the reserved mushroom mixture, the grated Parmesan, flat leaf parsley, salt and pepper. Mix well. Remove from the heat, cover and leave to rest for 2 minutes. Spoon into warmed bowls, top with Parmesan shavings and serve.

This party version of the Anglo-Indian dish from the days of the Raj is based on lightly smoked salmon, which gives it a luxurious flavour. You can use organic salmon and add a bit of smoked salmon at the end.

smoked salmon kedgeree

3 large eggs

250 g/8 oz. undyed skinless, boneless smoked haddock or cod fillet

250 g/8 oz. lightly smoked skinless, boneless salmon fillet or ordinary salmon fillet

3 tablespoons sunflower oil or other light oil

1 onion, finely chopped

2–3 teaspoons good-quality mild curry powder or pilau rice seasoning

300 g/1½ cups basmati rice

175 g/6 oz. cooked peeled prawns/ shrimp, thawed if frozen

40 g/3 tablespoons soft butter

2–3 tablespoons freshly squeezed lemon juice

3 heaped tablespoons chopped fresh coriander/cilantro leaves, plus a few whole leaves for decoration

sea salt and freshly ground black pepper

serves 6

Boil the eggs in a small saucepan of boiling water for 10–12 minutes depending on the size of the eggs. Drain off the water, pour cold running water over the eggs, then leave to cool in cold water.

Put the smoked haddock and salmon into a larger pan, just cover with cold water and bring gradually to the boil. Once bubbling, take off the heat and cover with a lid or foil. Leave for 5 minutes, then carefully remove the fish. Reserve 600 ml/2½ cups of the cooking water and set aside.

Heat the oil in a heavy-based pan or casserole and fry the onion over a moderate heat for about 6–7 minutes until starting to turn dark brown at the edges. Sprinkle in the curry powder or rice seasoning to taste. Add the rice, stir again and pour in the reserved cooking water. Bring to the boil then turn the heat right down and cover the pan. Cook for about 15–20 minutes until all the liquid has been absorbed.

Meanwhile, shell and quarter the eggs. Set aside 6 quarters and roughly chop the rest. Flake the fish carefully, removing any bones. Once the rice is cooked, fork it through and tip in the cooked fish, prawns/shrimp and eggs, cover the pan and leave for 5 minutes on a very low heat. Turn off the heat, add the butter, season with the lemon juice and a little salt and pepper and fork through the chopped coriander/cilantro. Serve on a warm platter decorated with the quartered eggs and the remaining coriander/cilantro leaves.

Note Keep covered in the pan for about 15–20 minutes before serving, or transfer to a very low oven and keep it for about 30–40 minutes.

Pumpkin isn't always held in the same high regard as other squash family members. Roasted pumpkin retains its deep flavour and unique texture here as it's roasted separately, then added to a basic risotto.

pumpkin & gorgonzola risotto

500 g/1 lb. pumpkin, peeled and cubed

1 tablespoon light olive oil

1 litre/4 cups vegetable stock

2 tablespoons butter

1 leek, halved lengthways and thinly sliced

1 garlic clove, chopped

330 g/1½ cups risotto rice, such as vialone nano, carnaroli or arborio

50 g/2 oz. Gorgonzola cheese, crumbled

serves 4

Preheat the oven to 180°C (350°F) Gas 4.

Put the pumpkin on a baking sheet, drizzle with the olive oil and roast in the preheated oven for 30 minutes.

Put the stock in a saucepan and heat until gently simmering. Melt the butter in a saucepan over high heat and add the leek and garlic. Cook for 4–5 minutes, stirring often, until the leeks have softened but not browned.

Add the rice to the leeks and stir for 1 minute, until the rice is well coated with oil. Add 125 ml/½ cup of the hot stock to the rice and cook, stirring constantly, until the rice has absorbed most of the liquid. Repeat this process until all the stock has been used, about 20–25 minutes. The rice should be soft but still have a slight bite to the centre.

Add the roasted pumpkin pieces. Remove the pan from the heat, stir in the Gorgonzola and serve immediately.

This sauce should be sweet and fruity so is a perfect way to use up soft, over-ripe tomatoes. Use a light olive oil; extra virgin burns at a lower temperature and will make the aubergine/eggplant bitter.

baked ziti with aubergine, basil & ricotta

400 g/14 oz. ziti, or other large tube-shaped pasta, such as rigatoni

185 ml/¾ cup light olive oil

1 aubergine/eggplant, halved and cut into very thin slices

1 onion, chopped

2 garlic cloves, chopped

3 tomatoes, chopped

1 small handful of fresh basil leaves, torn

125 ml/½ cup red wine

125 g/4 oz. ricotta cheese

45 g/½ cup pecorino cheese, grated

sea salt and freshly ground black pepper

a large ovenproof baking dish

serves 4

Preheat the oven to 220°C (425°F) Gas 7. Cook the pasta according to the package instructions. Drain well and return to the warm pan.

Heat the olive oil in a frying pan/skillet and when it is hot but not smoking, cook the aubergine/eggplant slices, in batches, for 2 minutes on each side, until golden. Remove and place on paper towels. Repeat to cook all of the aubergine/eggplant.

Pour off all but 1 tablespoon of oil from the frying pan/skillet, add the onion and garlic and cook for 2–3 minutes, stirring often. Add the tomatoes, basil and red wine, 250 ml/1 cup water, sea salt and black pepper to taste and bring to the boil. Boil for 10 minutes, until you have a thickened sauce. Stir in the aubergine/eggplant, then add to the pasta and stir well.

Put the mixture in the baking dish. Spoon the ricotta on top, sprinkle over the pecorino and bake in the preheated oven for 20 minutes until golden and crispy around the edges.

Polpetti — Italian meatballs — seem to use a lot of breadcrumbs. The bread lightens them and absorbs much more of the sauce and flavoursome oil released by the meat. A simple tomato sauce is all that's needed.

beef polpetti with spaghetti

300–400 g/10–12 oz. spaghetti

salt and freshly ground black pepper

tomato sauce

4 tablespoons/¼ cup extra virgin olive oil

3 garlic cloves, peeled and thinly sliced

1 large onion, cut into wedges

2 x 400-g/14-oz. cans chopped plum tomatoes

a handful fresh basil, plus extra to serve

meatballs

250 g/8 oz. minced/ground beef

100 g/1 cup fresh white breadcrumbs

2 eggs

25 g/2 tablespoons freshly grated Parmesan cheese, plus extra to serve

4 tablespoons/¼ cup chopped fresh parsley

3 tablespoons extra virgin olive oil

serves 4

To make the tomato sauce, put the olive oil, garlic, onion, tomatoes and basil in a saucepan, season well and bring to the boil. Reduce the heat and simmer gently for at least 40 minutes while you make the meatballs.

Preheat the oven to 200°C (400°F) Gas 6.

To make the meatballs, put the beef, breadcrumbs, eggs, Parmesan, parsley and olive oil in a large mixing bowl, season and combine with your hands. Shape the mixture into roughly 20 walnut-sized balls and put in a single layer on a baking sheet covered with foil. Roast for 10 minutes, turn, then roast for a further 6–7 minutes.

Put a saucepan of salted water on to boil for the spaghetti. When it comes to the boil, drop in the spaghetti and cook according to the package instructions until al dente. Drain, return to the pan and add the tomato sauce and meatballs. Stir very gently so as not to break up the meatballs. Take out the onion wedges if you prefer. Transfer to bowls and sprinkle with basil and grated Parmesan.

Macaroni cheese is a perennial favourite. Here it's given a modern makeover with upmarket cheeses like mascarpone and Parmesan, and a touch of garlic. The crisp topping rounds out the texture.

wicked macaroni cheese

60 g/½ cup fresh, chunky breadcrumbs

1 tablespoon olive oil

2 tablespoons butter

1 garlic clove, finely chopped

1 teaspoon dry mustard

3 tablespoons plain/all-purpose flour

500 ml/2 cups whole milk

125 ml/½ cup mascarpone

130 g/1 cup grated mature/sharp Cheddar cheese

60 g/½ cup grated Parmesan cheese

350 g/12 oz. macaroni

salt and freshly ground black pepper

a 21 x 21-cm/8 x 8-inch baking dish or 4 ramekins

serves 4

Preheat the oven to 200°C (400°F) Gas 6.

Spread the breadcrumbs on a baking sheet, drizzle with the oil and season. Bake for 6 minutes, remove and set aside.

Melt the butter in a saucepan. Add the garlic and mustard and sauté for 1 minute before adding the flour. Whisk constantly over medium heat until it forms a paste. Gradually whisk in the milk and turn up the heat. Bring to the boil, whisking constantly. Turn the heat down to low and simmer for 10 minutes. Remove from the heat and add the mascarpone, Cheddar and half of the Parmesan.

Boil the pasta in salted water until just al dente, drain and mix with the cheese sauce. Season and spoon the mixture into the baking dish or ramekins. Top with the breadcrumbs and with the remaining Parmesan. Bake for 20 minutes until golden. Stand for 5 minutes before serving.

For a really good pizza dough, use superfine durum wheat 'oo' flour, available in Italian stores and large supermarkets. If you wish you can add flavourings such as chopped herbs or grated cheese to the dough.

basic pizza dough

250g/2⅓ cups strong white bread flour, plus extra for sprinkling

½ teaspoon table salt

7-g/¼ oz. sachet fast-action dried yeast

2 tablespoons olive oil, plus extra to coat

125 ml/½ cup tepid water

makes 1 large pizza base

Put the flour, salt and yeast in a large bowl and mix. Make a well in the centre. Add the oil and water to the well and gradually work in the flour to make a soft dough. Sprinkle over a little flour if the mixture feels too sticky, but make sure it is not too dry either: the dough should be pliable and smooth.

Transfer the dough to a lightly floured surface. Knead for 10 minutes, sprinkling with a little more flour when needed, until the dough is smooth and stretchy.

Rub some oil over the surface of the dough and return the dough to the bowl. Cover with a clean kitchen cloth and leave for about 1 hour, until the dough has doubled in size.

Remove the dough to a lightly floured surface and knead for 2 minutes, until the excess air is knocked out. Roll out the dough according to the recipe you are following.

Variation To make a polenta base, use 50 g/½ cup fine polenta or cornmeal and 200 g/1½ cup strong white bread flour.

Note If you are in a real hurry, there are some good-quality package dough mixes available. Follow the instructions on the packet, but remember to roll it out very thinly.

A super-thick pizza with a deep crust you can really sink your teeth into. To be sure of a crisp base, cook this in a proper pizza pan, which has holes in the bottom to allow the steam to escape.

chicago deep-pan pepperoni pizza

double recipe Basic Pizza Dough (page 72)

2 tablespoons olive oil

½ recipe Tomato Sauce (page 68)

1 large tomato, sliced

1 small red onion, sliced and separated into rings

150 g/6 oz. mozzarella cheese, drained and sliced

100 g/4 oz. sliced pepperoni

sea salt and freshly ground black pepper

makes 1 x 30-cm/12-inch pizza

Preheat the oven to 200°C (400°F) Gas 6.

Roll out the dough on a lightly floured surface to 30-cm/12-inch diameter and push into a pizza pan or put onto a pizza stone or baking sheet. Brush with 1 tablespoon of the oil and spoon over the tomato sauce.

Arrange the tomato slices over the sauce. Lay the onion rings on top, splash over the remaining oil and sprinkle with salt and plenty of black pepper. Put into the preheated oven and cook for 20 minutes.

Remove from the oven and arrange the mozzarella and pepperoni slices over the top. Return the pizza to the oven and cook for a further 10–15 minutes, until risen and golden. Cut into wedges and serve.

Spinach and egg pizzas are popular in pizza restaurants everywhere, and you can easily make them, albeit in batches, at home. It doesn't matter if the yolk is a bit hard, but make sure that it goes onto the pizza whole.

fiorentina pizza

350 g/3 cups young spinach leaves

1 tablespoon butter

2 garlic cloves, crushed

1 recipe Basic Pizza Dough (page 72)

1–2 tablespoons olive oil

1 recipe Tomato Sauce (page 68)

150 g/6 oz. mozzarella cheese, drained and thinly sliced

4 small eggs

50 g/½ cup fontina or Gruyère cheese, finely grated

sea salt and freshly ground black pepper

makes 4 x 17-cm/9-inch pizzas

Put 2 baking sheets in the oven and preheat the oven to 220°C (425°F) Gas 7.

Wash the spinach thoroughly and put into a large saucepan. Cover with a lid and cook for 2–3 minutes, until the spinach wilts. Drain well and, when the spinach is cool enough to handle, squeeze out any excess water with your hands.

Melt the butter in a frying pan/skillet and cook the garlic for 1 minute. Add the drained spinach and cook for a further 3–4 minutes. Add salt and pepper to taste.

Divide the dough into 4, put on a lightly floured surface and roll out each piece to about 17 cm/9 inches in diameter. Brush with a little oil and spoon over the tomato sauce. Put the spinach on the bases, leaving a space in the middle for the egg. Put the mozzarella on top of the spinach, drizzle with a little more oil and sprinkle with salt and plenty of black pepper.

Carefully transfer 2 to the hot baking sheets and cook for 10 minutes. Remove from the oven and crack an egg into the middle of each pizza. Top with half the fontina or Gruyère and return to the oven for a further 5–10 minutes, until the base is crisp and golden and the eggs have just set. Slice and serve immediately, and cook the remaining 2 in the same way – they'll be ready to eat when the first are finished.

Roasting peppers is a lovely way to bring out their sweetness. Make sure the peppers are still warm when you add the flesh to the dressing, so that they absorb the flavours of the garlic and parsley.

roasted pepper pizza

2 red (bell) peppers

2 yellow (bell) peppers

2 garlic cloves, finely chopped

a small bunch of flat leaf parsley, finely chopped

2 tablespoons olive oil

1 recipe Basic Pizza Dough (page 72)

1 recipe Tomato Sauce (page 68)

150 g/about 2 cups tomatoes, sliced or halved

150 g/6 oz. mozzarella cheese, drained and sliced

sea salt and freshly ground black pepper

makes 1 x 30-cm/12-inch pizza

Put a pizza stone or baking sheet in the oven and preheat the oven to 220°C (425°F) Gas 7.

Put the (bell) peppers in a small roasting pan and bake in the preheated oven for about 30 minutes, turning occasionally, until the skin blisters and blackens.

Meanwhile, put the garlic and parsley in a bowl. Add the oil and salt and pepper to taste.

Remove the peppers from the oven, cover with a clean kitchen cloth and set aside for about 10 minutes, until cool enough to handle but still warm. Pierce the bottom of each pepper and squeeze the juices into the parsley and oil mixture. Skin and deseed the peppers. Cut the flesh into 2-cm/¾-inch strips and add to the mixture. Cover and set aside at room temperature until needed.

Roll out the dough on a lightly floured surface to 30-cm/12-inch diameter and brush with a little oil. Spoon over the tomato sauce and arrange the tomatoes and mozzarella on top. Spoon the pepper mixture over the top.

Carefully transfer to the hot pizza stone or baking sheet and cook for 20–25 minutes, until crisp and golden. Cut into wedges and serve.

These fish cakes are packed with fish and are free of additives. If using fresh fish, make double quantities and freeze half after shaping. You can also grill/broil or bake them in the oven until golden brown.

fish cakes & lemony beans

400 g/14 oz. potatoes, cut into large chunks

500 g/1 lb. white fish fillet such as cod loin or haddock, or salmon fillet

300 ml/1½ cups milk

a handful of fresh flat leaf parsley sprigs

1 bay leaf

1 tablespoon finely grated unwaxed lemon zest

2 tablespoons chopped fresh herbs, such as dill, parsley or coriander/cilantro

2–3 tablespoons wholemeal/whole-wheat flour

2–3 tablespoons sunflower oil

sea salt and freshly ground black pepper

lemony green beans

150 g/5 oz. green beans

1 tablespoon freshly squeezed lemon juice

1 tablespoon extra virgin olive oil

makes 8 small fish cakes

Cook the potatoes in a large saucepan of boiling water for 15 minutes until tender. Drain and mash.

Meanwhile, rinse the fish and put it in a frying pan/skillet with the milk, parsley sprigs and bay leaf. Bring to the boil, then cover and simmer for about 10 minutes until the fish is cooked and the flesh looks white. Remove the fish with a slotted spoon and transfer it to a large bowl. Let it cool slightly and when cool enough to handle, remove the skin and any bones and flake the flesh. Discard the cooking liquor.

Add the mashed potato, lemon zest and chopped herbs to the fish. Season to taste with salt and pepper, then mix lightly. Using your hands, shape the mixture into 8 small fish cakes. Put the flour on a plate and coat the fish cakes in it. Transfer the fish cakes to a plate, cover lightly with clingfilm/plastic wrap and chill in the refrigerator for at least 30 minutes.

To make the lemony green beans, lightly steam the beans for about 5 minutes until cooked but still slightly crunchy. Drain well, transfer to a warmed serving bowl and add the lemon juice, olive oil and a sprinkling of salt. Toss well and cover to keep warm.

To cook the fish cakes, heat the sunflower oil in a frying pan/skillet. Add the fish cakes and cook for 4–5 minutes on each side until golden brown, crisp and piping hot. Serve immediately with the lemony green beans.

Protein, essential fatty acids, calcium, iron, fibre — you name it, this fish pie has it. This is a particularly good meal for children since every mouthful will help build fitter, stronger, healthier little bodies.

individual fish pies

500 g/1 lb. potatoes, cut into large chunks

500 g/1 lb. cod or haddock fillet

400 ml/1¾ cups milk

1 bay leaf

250 g/8 oz. canned mackerel fillets in oil or tuna in spring water, drained

2 hard-boiled/-cooked eggs, roughly chopped

200 g/6 oz. baby spinach leaves

150 g/1½ cups frozen peas

5 tablespoons sunflower oil

4 tablespoons/¼ cup plain/all-purpose flour

1 large leek, thinly sliced

50 g/½ cup grated Cheddar cheese, (optional)

sea salt and freshly ground black pepper

8 x 150-ml/⅔-cup ramekins

serves 6–8

Cook the potatoes in a large saucepan of boiling water for 15 minutes until tender. Drain and mash. Preheat the oven to 190°C (375°F) Gas 5.

Rinse the cod or haddock and put it in a frying pan/skillet. Add the milk and bay leaf and bring to the boil. Reduce to a simmer and cook for 10 minutes. Remove from the heat and strain off and reserve the cooking liquor. When the fish has cooled, remove the skin and any bones, then flake it. Flake the mackerel and add it to the cooked fish with the chopped eggs.

Meanwhile, steam the spinach and peas for 3 minutes. Squeeze out any excess water from the spinach and chop it. Stir the spinach and peas into the fish mixture, then divide it between the ramekins.

Make the reserved cooking liquor up to 400 ml/1⅔ cups, if necessary, with more milk or water. Heat 4 tablespoons of the oil in a small saucepan and stir in the flour. Cook over low heat, stirring continuously, for 2 minutes. Remove the pan from the heat and gradually stir in the reserved cooking liquor. Return the pan to the heat and cook, stirring continuously, until the sauce thickens. Season to taste with salt and pepper, then pour the sauce over the fish in the ramekins.

Heat the remaining oil in a frying pan/skillet. Add the sliced leek and cook for 5 minutes until softened. Divide the leeks between the ramekins, then top each one with the mashed potato. Sprinkle the tops with a little grated cheese, if using. Bake in the preheated oven for 20–25 minutes until golden brown and bubbling and serve immediately.

A great supper dish, which is simple and quick, and makes a nice substantial meal with the beans and leeks. The Mustard and Tarragon butter is also delicious served with pan-fried or grilled/broiled salmon.

pan-fried chicken with creamy beans & leeks

4 boneless chicken breasts

25 g/2 tablespoons butter

1 tablespoon extra virgin olive oil

4 rounds Mustard and Tarragon Butter (see note)

sea salt and freshly ground black pepper

watercress salad, to serve

creamy beans and leeks

50 g/4 tablespoons butter

2 leeks, finely chopped

1 garlic clove, crushed

2 teaspoons chopped fresh rosemary

2 x 400-g/14-oz cans flageolet/cannellini beans, drained and rinsed

300 ml/1¼ cups vegetable stock

4 tablespoons/¼ cup double/heavy cream

serves 4

To cook the beans and leeks, melt the butter in a saucepan, add the leeks, garlic and rosemary and fry gently for 5 minutes until softened but not golden. Add the beans, stir once, then pour in the stock. Bring to the boil, cover and simmer for 15 minutes.

Remove the lid, stir in the cream, add salt and pepper to taste, then simmer, uncovered, for a further 5 minutes until the sauce has thickened. Set aside while you prepare the chicken.

Season the chicken with salt and pepper. Heat the butter and oil in a frying pan/skillet and as soon as the butter stops foaming, cook the chicken skin-side down for 4 minutes, turn over and cook for a further 4 minutes or until cooked through.

Top each breast with a couple of slices of the Mustard and Tarragon Butter and leave to rest for 2–3 minutes in a warm oven. Serve with the beans and a simple watercress salad.

Note To make the Mustard and Tarragon Butter, mix 2 tablespoons of chopped fresh tarragon with 125 g/1¼ sticks softened butter and 1 tablespoon wholegrain mustard. Roll, wrap in clingfilm/plastic wrap and freeze. To serve, slice off rounds as required.

Easy to prepare, these sage-crumbed pork chops are served with Irish-style colcannon: creamy mashed potato with cooked cabbage. This recipe uses kale, a close cabbage relative, and a true cold weather veg.

sage pork chops with kale colcannon mash

60 g/½ cup plain/all-purpose flour

3 eggs

2 tablespoons Worcestershire sauce

4–6 fresh sage leaves, finely chopped

100 g/1 cup fresh breadcrumbs

100 g/1 cup Parmesan cheese, finely grated

4 pork chops

60 ml/¼ cup vegetable oil

kale colcannon

500 g/1 lb. curly kale

2 tablespoons butter

2 slices of bacon, thinly sliced

6–8 spring onions/scallions, thinly sliced

4 large potatoes, quartered

125 g/1 stick butter, cut into cubes

serves 4

Put the flour on a flat plate. Mix the eggs and Worcestershire sauce in a bowl and, in a separate bowl, combine the sage, breadcrumbs and Parmesan. Press a pork chop into the flour, coating the meat evenly, then dip it in the egg mixture, then press firmly to coat in the crumb mix. Repeat this process with all 4 pork chops. Transfer them to a plate and refrigerate until needed.

To make the colcannon, cook the kale in a large saucepan of boiling water for 5 minutes. Drain well, chop finely and set aside. Put the butter in a frying pan/skillet over medium heat. Add the bacon and cook for 5 minutes, stirring occasionally until it turns golden. Add the spring onions/scallions and cook for a further 2 minutes. Stir in the kale and take the pan off the heat.

Boil the potatoes for 20 minutes, until soft but not breaking apart. Drain well and return them to the pan. Add the butter and mash well. Beat with a wooden spoon until smooth. Stir the kale mixture into the potatoes, cover and keep warm while cooking the pork.

Heat the vegetable oil in a large frying pan/skillet over medium heat. When hot, add the pork chops and cook gently for 6–7 minutes, so that a golden crust forms. Turn over the pork chops and cook for 5 minutes on the other side. Serve with a generous portion of the kale colcannon.

Adults and children alike enjoy this classic dish, which is also known as pigs-in-a-blanket. Choose your favourite sausages, and serve individual ones as a treat for the whole family.

toad-in-the-hole

115 g/¾ cup plain/all-purpose flour

2 large eggs

250 ml/1 cup milk

a small bunch of fresh chives, snipped into 3-cm/1-inch pieces

12 tiny chipolata/breakfast link sausages or cocktail sausages, or 6 larger sausages cut in half

4 tablespoons/¼ cup vegetable oil

sea salt and freshly ground black pepper

a 12-hole non-stick muffin pan

makes 12 individual portions

Preheat the oven to 220°C (425°F) Gas 7, and put a large baking sheet or roasting pan under the middle shelf to catch any drips.

To make the batter, put the flour and a pinch each of salt and pepper in a large bowl. Make a hollow in the centre, then break the eggs into the hollow. Pour the milk into the hollow. Whisk together the eggs and milk, and start to mix the flour into the hollow. When all the flour has been mixed in, whisk the batter well to get rid of any lumps. Add the snipped chives and whisk them into the batter. Transfer the batter to a large jug/pitcher. (The batter can be made up to 3 hours before you start cooking.)

Put 1 teaspoon of oil into each hole of the muffin pan and heat in the oven for 5 minutes. Remove from the oven and put 1 chipolata or half sausage in each hole, and return to the oven for 5 minutes.

Remove the hot pan as before, stir the batter briefly, and pour some into each hole so that it is half full. Return the pan to the oven and bake for 20 minutes until golden brown and crispy.

Remove from the oven and ease each portion out of its hole. Eat straight away with salad or green vegetables or even baked beans.

Sweet potatoes and lentils are low glycaemic index foods, which means they release their sugars into the blood stream at a slow, steady rate, keeping energy levels constant. Comfort food without the guilt.

baked sweet potatoes with cheesy lentil hash & bacon

4 sweet potatoes, about 100 g/3½ oz. each

200 g/1 cup red split lentils

450–500 ml/2–2½ cups vegetable stock

1–2 garlic cloves, crushed

1 onion, very finely chopped

2 celery ribs/stalks, very thinly sliced

1 tablespoon soy sauce

2 tablespoons tomato purée/paste

6 slices of lean back bacon, grilled/broiled and chopped

100 g/¾ cup extra-mature/sharp Cheddar cheese, grated

serves 4

Preheat the oven to 200°C (400°F) Gas 6.

Lightly prick the sweet potatoes with a fork and bake directly on the oven shelves for 35–40 minutes until soft when gently squeezed. Remove and leave until cool enough to handle.

Meanwhile, put the lentils in a saucepan, add the stock and bring to the boil. Cover, reduce the heat and simmer for 20–25 minutes until soft. Add more stock or water if the lentils start to dry out.

About 10 minutes before the lentils are done, put the garlic, onion, celery, soy sauce and 3–4 tablespoons water in a non-stick frying pan/skillet and heat gently for about 10 minutes or until the vegetables are soft. Add them to the saucepan of cooked lentils along with the tomato purée/paste, chopped grilled/broiled bacon and half the grated cheese. Mix well, then reheat gently, stirring occasionally, until hot.

Preheat the grill/broiler. Cut the cooked sweet potatoes in half. Put them in an ovenproof dish and top with the lentil mixture. Sprinkle with the remaining cheese and cook under a preheated hot grill/broiler for 10 minutes or until the cheese is golden and bubbling. Serve hot.

Traditional potato rösti, served in wedges, are crispy and hearty. Add grated celeriac to them: like celery, but sweeter, it gives a base note that enhances the flavour of the other ingredients it is cooked with.

sausages with winter rösti

8 good-quality organic pork sausages

2 tablespoons olive oil

Dijon mustard, to serve

winter rösti

3 potatoes, unpeeled and halved

1 small head of celeriac (about 800 g/1¾ lbs.), peeled and quartered

3 tablespoons butter

3 tablespoons olive oil

sea salt and freshly ground black pepper

serves 4

To make the rösti, put the potatoes and celeriac in a saucepan and cover with cold water. Bring to the boil, then immediately remove from the heat and cover with a tight-fitting lid. Set aside for 10 minutes. Drain well and leave to cool completely.

Grate the potatoes and celeriac into a bowl with 1 teaspoon sea salt and some black pepper. Toss to combine. Heat half of the butter and 1 tablespoon of the oil in a large non-stick frying pan/skillet over high heat, swirling the butter around to coat the bottom of the pan. Add the potato mixture and gently press down to form a large cake. Cook for 5 minutes over high heat. Pour 1 tablespoon of olive oil around the very edge of the pan and gently shake the pan often to prevent the rösti from sticking to the bottom. Reduce the heat to medium and cook for 10 minutes, shaking the pan often.

Take a plate slightly larger than the pan. Place it on top of the pan, then carefully invert the rösti onto the plate. Add the remaining oil and butter to the pan, then carefully slide the rösti back into the pan, cooked side up, and cook for 10 minutes.

Meanwhile, to cook the sausages, heat the oil in a frying pan/skillet over medium heat. Prick the sausages with a fork, add them to the pan and cook for 20 minutes, turning often, to cook an even golden brown. Cut the rösti and spoon directly from the pan onto serving plates. Serve with the sausages and a little mustard on the side.

For a burger to be truly 'all American' it must be served in a sesame-seed bun with lettuce, tomato, American mustard and dill pickles, and it must have French fries on the side.

classic all-american hamburger with french fries

750 g/1½ lbs. minced/ground beef

1 onion, finely chopped

1 teaspoon Worcestershire sauce

4 sesame-seed buns, halved

2 tablespoons American/yellow mustard, plus extra to serve

100 g/1 cup shredded lettuce leaves

2 tomatoes, sliced

2 dill pickles, sliced

sea salt and freshly ground black pepper

olive oil, for brushing

French fries, to serve

serves 4

Put the beef, onion, Worcestershire sauce and some salt and pepper in a bowl and work together with your hands until evenly mixed. Divide the mixture into 4 portions and shape into patties. Cover and chill in the refrigerator for 30 minutes.

Preheat the grill/broiler if using. Brush the patties lightly with olive oil and barbecue or grill/broil for 4–5 minutes on each side until lightly charred and just cooked through inside.

Meanwhile, toast the buns and spread one half of each with mustard. Add the shredded lettuce, patties, tomato slices and dill pickles, squeeze over a little extra mustard and add the bun tops. Serve at once with French fries.

This is the ultimate American-style hot sandwich and guaranteed to be a hit with anyone who enjoys a good steak. The home-made mustard mayonnaise tastes particularly good so it's worth the effort.

steak sandwich with french fries

4 tablespoons olive oil, plus extra for brushing

2 onions, thinly sliced

750 g/1½ lbs. sirloin steaks

4 small baguettes, halved lengthways

8 tablespoons/½ cup Home-made Mustard Mayonnaise (see note)

100 g/4 oz. watercress leaves

sea salt and freshly ground black pepper

French fries, to serve

serves 4

Heat the oil in a frying pan/skillet, add the onions, season with salt and pepper and fry over medium heat for 20–25 minutes until golden and caramelized. Set aside and keep them warm.

Brush the steaks with olive oil and season liberally with salt and pepper. Preheat a heavy frying pan/skillet until hot and fry the steaks for 3 minutes on each side for rare, 4 minutes for medium and 5 minutes for well done. Leave to rest for 5 minutes, then slice thickly.

Meanwhile, lightly toast the baguettes and spread the insides liberally with mustard mayonnaise. Fill with watercress leaves, the sliced beef and all the juices and top with the onions. Serve hot with French fries.

Note Home-made mayonnaise has a far nicer flavour and consistency than bought versions and using a food processor makes the job simple. Put 3 very fresh egg yolks, 2 teaspoons Dijon mustard and 2 teaspoons white wine vinegar or freshly squeezed lemon juice in a food processor and blend briefly until foaming. With the motor running, gradually pour in 300 ml/1¼ cups olive oil through the funnel until the mixture is thick and glossy. Season to taste with sea salt and transfer to a bowl and cover with clingfilm/plastic wrap. Refrigerate for up to 3 days and use as required.

bakes,
casseroles & roasts

Parsley, chives, chervil and tarragon make up the *fines herbes* of French cooking and they like being in a dish throughout the cooking process. Do try this pastry recipe at least once before resorting to frozen pastry.

chicken, leek & tarragon pot pie

3 tablespoons butter

750 g/1½ lbs. chicken thigh fillets, cut into bite-sized pieces

4 medium leeks (white parts only), thickly sliced

3 tablespoons plain/all-purpose flour

250 ml/1 cup chicken stock

125 ml/½ cup single/light cream

2 tablespoons finely chopped fresh tarragon

2 tablespoons roughly chopped fresh flat leaf parsley

sea salt and freshly ground black pepper

pie pastry

185 g/1½ cups plain/all-purpose flour

2 tablespoons butter

2 tablespoons sour cream

1 egg, lightly beaten

a 1.5-litre/3-quart ovenproof pie dish

serves 4

To make the pastry, process the flour, butter and a pinch of salt for a few seconds. With the motor running, add the sour cream, half of the beaten egg and 1–2 tablespoons cold water, until the dough comes together. Roll into a ball, wrap in clingfilm/plastic wrap and chill for 30 minutes.

Preheat the oven to 180°C (350°F) Gas 4. Heat half of the butter in a frying pan/skillet over high heat. When sizzling, brown the chicken for 2–3 minutes, turning often. Transfer to a bowl. Add the remaining butter to the pan and cook the leeks over medium heat for 2 minutes. Cover with a lid, reduce the heat, and cook for 2–3 minutes until really softened.

Return the chicken to the pan and increase the heat to high. Sprinkle in the flour and cook for 2 minutes, stirring constantly so the flour thickly coats the chicken and leeks. Gradually add the stock, stirring all the time. Bring to the boil, then stir in the cream, tarragon and parsley. Season well. Reduce heat and simmer until thickened, about 1 minute. Remove from the heat and cool. Spoon into the pie dish.

Place the dough between 2 pieces of wax paper and roll out to a thickness of 5 mm/¼ inch, making sure the dough is more than big enough to cover the dish. Place the dough over the top of the pie, leaving the edges to overhang. Cut several slits in the top of the pie and gently press around the edges with a fork. Brush the remaining beaten egg over the top. Put the pie dish on a baking sheet and cook in the preheated oven for 30 minutes, until the pastry is golden.

Autumn/fall is a great time for pies. The weather is typically fickle and a pie gives you the option of serving a slice with creamy mash if it's chilly or a late-season tomato salad and a tangy dressing if it's not.

egg, bacon & spinach pie

500 g/1 lb. fresh spinach, washed

1 tablespoon butter

3 slices of rindless bacon, cut into thin strips

1 onion, finely chopped

6 eggs, lightly beaten

50 g/½ cup Parmesan cheese, finely grated

1 egg, lightly beaten with 1 tablespoon cold water

shortcrust pastry

250 g/2 cups plain/all-purpose flour

150 g/1 stick plus 2 tablespoons butter, cubed

1 egg yolk

a loose-based tart pan, 20-cm/8-inch diameter, lightly greased

serves 6

To make the pastry, put the flour and butter into a bowl and freeze for 15 minutes. Lightly beat the egg yolk with 2 tablespoons water and chill for 15 minutes. Process the butter and flour until the mixture looks like ground almonds, then add the egg yolk mixture and process for just a few seconds to combine. Use your hands to bring the dough together to form one large crumbly ball. Wrap in clingfilm/plastic wrap and chill for 30 minutes.

Preheat the oven to 180°C (350°F) Gas 4.

Cook the wet spinach in a large non-stick frying pan/skillet over high heat for 2 minutes, until wilted and emerald-green in colour, in batches if necessary. Drain well. When cool enough to handle, use your hands to squeeze out as much moisture as possible from the spinach and place it in a large bowl.

Heat the butter in the frying pan/skillet over high heat and, when sizzling, add the bacon and onion. Cook for 5 minutes until golden. Spoon the mixture into the bowl with the spinach. Add the eggs and Parmesan and season well with sea salt and black pepper. Stir to combine.

Put the tart pan on a baking sheet. Cut about two-thirds from the ball of dough and roll it out between 2 layers of wax paper. Line the bottom of the tart pan with the pastry. Spoon the spinach mixture on top of the pastry base. Roll the remaining pastry into a circle slightly larger than the tart pan and place on top of the pie, allowing any excess pastry to hang over the edge. Gently press down the edges to seal. Brush the egg and water mixture over the pie and cook in the preheated oven for 1 hour until golden brown. Cool for 10–15 minutes.

If it is comfort food you're after, particularly when it's cold, nothing beats a good homemade pie with tender pieces of meat in a delicious mushroomy gravy. This one is topped with crisp suet pastry.

steak & mushroom pie

3 tablespoons olive oil

2 onions, chopped

750 g/1½ lbs. braising steak/ stewing beef, cubed

200 g/1¾ cups button mushrooms

1 tablespoon plain/all-purpose flour

½ teaspoon dried mixed herbs

1 teaspoon Worcestershire sauce

1 teaspoon English or Dijon mustard

400 ml/1¾ cups beef stock

sea salt and freshly ground black pepper

suet pastry

250 g/1⅔ cups self-raising/rising flour

125 g/4 oz. shredded suet or shortening

sea salt and freshly ground black pepper

a 1.2-litre/5-cup pie dish

serves 4

To make the filling, heat the olive oil in a large frying pan/skillet, add the onions and fry until softened and translucent. Transfer to a plate. Add a little more oil to the pan if needed, then add the meat and sauté until browned and sealed.

Add the mushrooms and fry for about 5 minutes, then sprinkle in the flour and mix well to absorb all the oil. Return the onions to the pan and add the mixed herbs, Worcestershire sauce, mustard, salt and pepper. Slowly pour in the stock, blending well. Bring to the boil, then lower the heat and simmer the mixture for 1½ hours.

When the meat is almost cooked, preheat the oven to 220°C (425°F) Gas 7 and make the pastry. Sift the flour into a bowl, add the suet or shortening, salt and pepper and mix well. Add about 5 tablespoons water and mix with a round-bladed knife until the mixture forms a dough. A little more water may be needed, but take care not to add too much as it will make the pastry difficult to handle. Transfer the cooked meat to the pie dish, and set aside to cool.

Roll out the pastry to a disc larger than the pie dish. Wet the lip of the dish, then cut thin strips of pastry from the trimmings and press onto the lip. Dampen this pastry lip. Lay the rolled pastry over the pie and flute the edge with your fingers to seal. Trim and make a small hole in the centre. Bake in the preheated oven for about 35 minutes, until golden brown.

The pot roast is one of the great American classics and when it appears with braised vegetables, it becomes Yankee Pot Roast. You can also roast the vegetables instead of braising them.

yankee pot roast with braised root vegetables

1 kg/2 lbs. rolled silverside/boneless beef chuck or rump roast, neatly tied

3 tablespoons oil or bacon fat

1 tablespoon ground allspice

1 teaspoon sea salt

2 tablespoons plain/all-purpose flour

1 tablespoon dry mustard

150 ml/²/₃ cup red wine

500 ml/2 cups beef stock

6 tablespoons butter

4 parsnips, cut into 5-cm/2-inch chunks

2 sweet potatoes, cut into 5-cm/2-inch chunks

2 carrots, cut into 5-cm/2-inch chunks

12 small red onions, cut into 4 wedges through the root

2 tablespoons cornflour/cornstarch

sea salt and freshly ground black pepper

an ovenproof casserole

Put the meat in a shallow dish. Put 1 tablespoon of the oil, allspice, salt, flour and mustard in a small bowl and mix to form a paste, adding more oil as necessary. Rub the meat with the mixture, cover and marinate in the refrigerator for 3 hours or overnight.

Preheat the oven to 180°C (350°F) Gas 4. Remove the meat and shake off any excess spices. Heat the remaining oil or bacon fat in a large frying pan/skillet, add the meat and brown on all sides. Transfer to an ovenproof casserole. Add the wine to the frying pan/skillet, bring to the boil and cook until reduced by two-thirds. Add the stock and bring to the boil, pour over the meat, cover with a lid and cook in the preheated oven for 1½ hours or until tender.

About 30 minutes before the meat is done, add the butter to the frying pan/skillet, heat gently, then add the vegetables and fry until they take on a little colour. Sprinkle with salt and pepper, cover with a lid and simmer in their own juices for 20 minutes. Keep them warm.

When the meat is cooked, drain off the liquid into a saucepan. Mix the cornflour/cornstarch with 3 tablespoons water and blend it into the liquid. Bring to the boil, then taste and adjust the seasoning. Pour the sauce back over the meat and vegetables and heat on top of the stove.

To serve, transfer the meat to a platter and arrange the reheated vegetables around. Serve the gravy separately.

This dish must be made in advance in order for the flavours to develop and the sauce to taste rich and delicious. To reheat it from cold, put into a preheated oven at 180°C (350°F) Gas 4 for 35 minutes.

daube of beef

1.75 kg/4 lb. rump of beef/
boneless rump roast

1 bottle white wine, 750 ml

2 bay leaves

4 tablespoons/¼ cup olive oil

2 onions, sliced

2 garlic cloves, crushed and chopped

3 tablespoons plain/all-purpose flour,
plus extra for dusting

1 tablespoon drained capers

100 g/4 oz. pitted black olives

a 400-g/14-oz. can chopped tomatoes

grated zest of ½ an unwaxed orange

200 g/8 oz. baby carrots

125 g/4 oz. button mushrooms

large bunch of flat leaf parsley,
chopped

sea salt and freshly ground
black pepper

egg noodle pasta or boiled potatoes,
to serve

a flameproof casserole

serves 6

Put the beef, wine, bay leaves, salt and pepper into a large bowl, cover and chill for 24 hours, turning the beef in its marinade from time to time.

Preheat the oven to 140°C (275°F) Gas 1.

Drain the beef, reserving the marinade, and pat dry with paper towels. Heat 2 tablespoons of the oil in a casserole dish, add the onions and garlic and cook gently for 8 minutes. Sprinkle with the flour and stir. Add the marinade liquid a little at a time, stirring constantly. Add the capers, olives, tomatoes and orange zest and simmer while you prepare the beef.

Put the remaining olive oil into a frying pan/skillet and heat until hot. Dust the beef in flour and add to the frying pan/skillet. Fry until brown on all sides, then transfer to the casserole. Put a few tablespoons of juice from the casserole back into the frying pan/skillet and stir to scrape up any meaty bits. Add the juice and bits back to the casserole.

Cover with a lid, transfer to the preheated oven and cook for 2 hours. Remove from the oven and add the carrots and mushrooms. Return the casserole to the oven and cook for 1 further hour.

Remove the beef to a board, slice thickly and serve on heated dinner plates. Stir the chopped parsley into the sauce and spoon the sauce and vegetables over the beef. Serve with egg noodle pasta, tossed in parsley and butter, or with boiled potatoes.

Apple and fennel puddings may sound unusual but packed as they are with vegetables and honey-sweet raisins, they make a wonderful alternative to roast vegetables as an accompaniment to roast pork.

roasted pork with apple & fennel puddings

1.5 kg/3½ lbs. piece of pork loin, skin on

2 tablespoons white wine vinegar

1 tablespoon sea salt

apple and fennel puddings

3 tablespoons butter

1 onion, chopped

1 celery rib/stalk, thinly sliced

1 green apple, grated

1 fennel bulb, grated

100 g/1 cup fresh breadcrumbs

60 g/⅓ cup raisins

1 egg, lightly beaten

250 ml/1 cup chicken stock

45 g/⅓ cup flaked/slivered almonds

a cooking rack
a large roasting pan
a baking dish, greased

serves 6

Make small incisions on the skin of the pork, 1 cm/½ inch apart but don't cut through to the meat. Rub the vinegar and sea salt into the skin and set aside for 1 hour at room temperature. (This will let the skin dry out making for better crackling.)

Preheat the oven to 220°C (425°F) Gas 7.

Put the pork on a cooking rack over a roasting pan. Pour 250 ml/1 cup water into the pan and cook in the preheated oven for 30 minutes. Reduce the oven temperature to 180°C (350°F) Gas 4 and cook for a further 1½ hours, until the pork skin is golden and crisp. Keep adding water to the roasting pan during the cooking time as necessary. Remove the pork from the oven, cover with foil and let rest for 10 minutes.

Meanwhile, make the puddings. Heat the butter in a frying pan/skillet over medium heat. When the butter is sizzling, add the onion and celery and cook for 4–5 minutes, stirring often. Add the apple and fennel and cook for 1 minute, stirring well. Remove the pan from the heat and add all the remaining ingredients, except for the almonds. Stir well. Spoon the mixture into the prepared baking dish, sprinkle the almonds on top and put the dish in the oven 1 hour before the end of the pork cooking time. Serve slices of the pork with wedges of the pudding.

Unlike roast pork, where the fat and skin form tasty crackling, excess fat on roast beef can be off-putting. Choose a trimmed, premium fillet, keep it lean and cook it quickly for a lovely rare roast.

roast beef with winter vegetables & garlic crème

800 g/1¾ lbs. beef rib-eye fillet/ boneless roast

1 tablespoon freshly ground black pepper

1 bunch of baby carrots, unpeeled and tops trimmed

2 small red onions, cut into thin wedges

1 turnip, cut into quarters

½ small celeriac, cut into batons

1 large parsnip, cut into semi circles

1 tablespoon light olive oil

garlic crème

1 head of garlic

3 egg yolks

1 teaspoon Dijon mustard

1 teaspoon red wine vinegar

250 ml/1 cup light olive oil

a large roasting pan

serves 4

To make the garlic crème, preheat the oven to 180°C (350°F) Gas 4. Wrap the garlic firmly in 2 layers of foil and cook in the preheated oven for 40 minutes. Remove and let cool.

Cut the garlic in half and squeeze the soft flesh directly into the bowl of a food processor. Add the egg yolks, mustard and vinegar and process until smooth. With the motor running, add the olive oil in a steady stream until all the oil is incorporated. Transfer to a bowl, cover and refrigerate until needed.

Put the beef in a bowl and rub the pepper all over it. Transfer to a plate and refrigerate, uncovered, for at least 3 hours or, ideally, overnight. When you are ready to cook, preheat the oven to 220°C (425°F) Gas 7 and put a baking sheet in the oven to heat up. Put the vegetables onto the baking sheet, drizzle with olive oil and roast for 30 minutes. Turn and roast for a further 10 minutes. Remove from the oven and keep warm.

Heat a non-stick frying pan/skillet over high heat. When smoking hot, sear the beef for 4 minutes, turning every minute. Put it in a roasting pan and roast in the preheated oven for 10 minutes. Turn the beef and cook for 5 minutes more. Remove from the oven, cover with foil and let rest for 10 minutes before carving into slices to serve with the garlic crème.

The affiliation between marmalade and ribs works very well, making messy, delicious finger food: have toothpicks, paper napkins and finger-bowls on hand. Longer slower cooking makes the meat more tender.

sticky spareribs with orange–chilli glaze

300 g/10 oz. fine-cut orange marmalade

325 g/1⅓ cups honey

4 tablespoons/¼ cup Worcestershire sauce

1 tablespoon soy sauce

freshly squeezed juice of 1 lime

1 teaspoon cayenne pepper

1 teaspoon ground ginger

1 teaspoon ground cumin

1 teaspoon dried oregano

½ teaspoon coarse salt

1.5 kg/3 lbs. spareribs

extra virgin olive oil

coarse sea salt

a large roasting pan

serves 4

To make the sauce, put the marmalade, honey, Worcestershire sauce, soy sauce, lime juice, cayenne, ginger, cumin, oregano and salt in a saucepan and stir well. Cook over low heat, stirring often, until the marmalade has melted completely. Set aside until needed.

Preheat the oven to 180°C (350°F) Gas 4.

Brush the ribs lightly with oil, and arrange in a roasting pan – slightly overlapping is fine – with the meaty side up. Cook in the preheated oven. Total cooking time is about 2 hours, but turn the ribs every 30 minutes for the first 1½ hours. After this time, baste the ribs with the sauce on both sides. Return to the pan, meat side down. Cook for 15 minutes, baste generously all over again, turn the ribs and cook for about 10 minutes more. Remove from the oven, slice into ribs and serve hot. (Be sure to soak the pan straight away.)

Variation For a shorter cooking time you can baste the ribs with half the sauce, then cover and refrigerate overnight. Preheat the oven to 200°C (400°F) Gas 6. Line a large roasting pan with foil. Put the ribs in the pan, meat side down, sprinkle with salt and cook for 30 minutes. Add a splash of water to the pan to keep from smoking, baste the ribs and turn. Cook in the oven at for 20 minutes more. Baste well all over, turn and cook for 5 minutes more. Slice ribs and serve hot.

This classic Tuscan dish re-creates the tastes and smells of the early-morning markets in your own kitchen. Use plenty of rosemary so that the pork flesh will be suffused with its aroma.

pork loin roasted with rosemary & garlic

1.75 kg/3 lbs. loin of pork on the bone*

6 large garlic cloves

4 tablespoons/¼ cup chopped fresh rosemary

300 ml/1¼ cups dry white wine

a few sprigs of fresh rosemary

olive oil, for brushing

sea salt and freshly ground black pepper

fine kitchen string

2 large roasting pans

serves 6

Turn the loin fat-side down. Make deep slits all over, especially in the thick part. Put the garlic, rosemary and at least 1 teaspoon of salt and pepper (more will give a truly authentic Tuscan flavour) into a food processor and blend to a paste. Push this paste into all the slits in the meat and spread the remainder over the surface of the meat. Roll up and tie with string.

Weigh the meat and calculate the cooking time, allowing 25 minutes for every 500 g/1 lb. At this stage you can cover with clingfilm/plastic wrap and chill for several hours to deepen the flavour. When ready to cook, preheat the oven to 230°C (450°F) Gas 8, or as high as your oven will go. Uncover the pork and brown all over in a hot frying pan/skillet. Set in a roasting pan. Pour the wine over the pork and tuck in the rosemary sprigs.

Put the bones in another roasting pan, convex side up. Rub the skin with a little oil and salt, then drape over the bones. Put the pan on the top shelf of the oven, and the pork loin on the bottom or middle shelf. Roast for 20 minutes. Turn down the heat to 200°C (400°F) Gas 6, and roast for the remaining calculated time, basting the pork loin every 20 minutes.

Rest the pork in a warm place for 15 minutes before carving into thick slices. Serve with shards of crunchy crackling and the pan juices.

* **Note** Ask the butcher to bone the loin (but to give you the bones) and to remove the skin and score it for crackling.

Brisket is a much-underrated cut with a rich flavour that lends itself well to braising. You can use any full-bodied red wine, but Zinfandel has just the right gutsy rustic character.

pot roast brisket with Zinfandel

200 ml/¾ cup Zinfandel or other full-bodied red wine

200 ml/¾ cup fresh beef stock or stock made with ½ a stock cube, cooled

2 tablespoons red wine vinegar

1 large garlic clove, crushed

1 bay leaf

1 onion, chopped

a few of sprigs of fresh thyme or ½ teaspoon dried thyme

1.5 kg/3½ lbs. boned, rolled brisket of beef

2–3 tablespoons sunflower or light olive oil

2 tablespoons dry Marsala or Madeira

sea salt and freshly ground pepper

a flameproof casserole dish

serves 6

Mix the wine and stock with the wine vinegar, garlic, bay leaf, onion and thyme. Put the meat in a sturdy plastic bag, pour over the marinade and pull the top of the bag together tightly so that the liquid covers the meat. Knot the top of the bag or seal with a wire tie. Let the meat marinate in the refrigerator for at least 4 hours or overnight.

Preheat the oven to 200°C (400°F) Gas 6.

Remove the meat from the marinade and dry thoroughly with paper towels. Strain the marinade and reserve the liquid. Heat the oil in a flameproof casserole dish. Brown the meat all over in the hot oil, then add 3–4 tablespoons of the strained marinade. Put a lid on the casserole and roast for 2 hours. Check from time to time that the pan juices are not burning. Add more marinade if necessary, but the flavour of this dish comes from the well-browned sticky juices, so do not add too much extra liquid. If on the other hand more liquid has formed, spoon some out. Simmer the remaining marinade over low heat until it loses its raw, winey taste.

Once the meat is cooked, set it aside in a warm place. Spoon any fat off the surface of the pan juices and add the Marsala and the cooked marinade. Bring to the boil, scraping off all the brown tasty bits from the side of the casserole and adding a little extra water if necessary. Season to taste with salt and pepper and serve spooned over slices of the meat or in a gravy boat for pouring.

Although Boeuf Bourguignon sounds as if it should be made from red Burgundy, just as good is a more full-bodied red from the Rhône or Languedoc. Make it a day ahead to allow the flavours to develop.

boeuf bourguignon

900 g/2 lbs. braising beef/beef chuck or steak

3 tablespoons olive oil

130 g/4½ oz. cubed pancetta

3 onions, finely chopped

2 large garlic cloves, finely chopped

1½ tablespoons plain/all-purpose flour

450 ml/2 cups full-bodied red wine, plus an extra splash if needed

a bouquet garni made from a few sprigs of thyme, parsley stalks and a bay leaf

25 g/2 tablespoons butter

250 g/4 oz. chestnut mushrooms, cleaned and halved

2 tablespoons finely chopped fresh flat leaf parsley

sea salt and freshly ground black pepper

apple sauce and boiled new potatoes, to serve

a flameproof casserole dish

serves 6

Pat the meat dry, trim off any excess fat or sinew and cut into large chunks. Heat 1 tablespoon of the oil in a frying pan/skillet and fry the pancetta until lightly browned. Remove from the pan with a slotted spoon and transfer to a flameproof casserole dish. Brown the meat in 2 batches in the fat that remains in the pan and add to the pancetta. Add the remaining oil and fry the onion slowly, covering the pan, until soft and caramelized (about 25 minutes), adding the garlic halfway through the cooking time.

Stir the flour into the onions, cook for a minute, then add the wine and bring to the boil. Pour over the meat, add the bouquet garni and bring back to the boil. Turn down the heat and simmer over very low heat for 2–2½ hours, until the meat is just tender.

Turn off the heat and leave the casserole overnight, if you wish. The next day bring the casserole back to boiling point, then turn down low again.

Heat the butter in a frying pan/skillet and fry the mushrooms until lightly browned (about 5 minutes). Tip the mushrooms into the stew, stir and cook for another 10–15 minutes. Season the casserole to taste with salt and pepper, adding an extra splash of wine if you don't think the flavour is quite pronounced enough. Sprinkle over chopped parsley before serving with apple sauce and boiled new potatoes or mashed potato.

Some fat is needed here to moisten the beans. A 'hand' of pork is part of the shoulder, and is good for roasting or braising, as it has the right amount of fat; the leg is so lean as to make it difficult to keep moist.

tuscan pork & bean casserole

250 g/1½ cups dried cannellini or great Northern beans

4 tablespoons/¼ cup olive oil

350 g/12 oz. carrots, cut into 3-cm/1-inch chunks

4 onions, peeled but left whole

4 small turnips

1 sprig of thyme

1 bay leaf

6 peppercorns

6 garlic cloves, or to taste

2 kg/4 lbs. hand/shoulder of pork

250 g/8 oz. thick-cut bacon, cut into chunks

750 g/1½ lbs. small potatoes, peeled

250 g/8 oz. fresh green beans

sea salt and freshly ground black pepper

a flameproof casserole dish

serves 4

Put the dried beans in a bowl, cover with water and let soak overnight. Drain, transfer the beans to a saucepan, cover with water again and bring to the boil. Drain and discard this water, reserving the beans to add to the stew.

Heat the oil in a casserole dish, then stir in the carrots, onions, turnips, thyme, bay leaf, peppercorns and garlic. Sauté gently until softened but not browned.

Meanwhile, preheat the oven to 170°C (325°F) Gas 3. Cut the rind off the pork and reserve it. Add the pork, its rind, the bacon chunks and the drained beans to the casserole. Cover with water, add salt and pepper and bring to the boil on top of the stove. Transfer to the preheated oven and simmer for 1½ hours, or until the beans are tender.

After 1 hour, taste and adjust the seasoning, then add the potatoes for the last 30 minutes and the fresh green beans for the last 5 minutes.

To serve, remove and discard the pork rind, lift the meat onto a dish and carve into thick slices. Add the vegetables and beans to the dish and serve with a separate small jug/pitcher of the cooking juices.

A traditional hotpot was an earthenware vessel with a tight-fitting lid, tall enough to take mutton cutlets standing upright. Nowadays, any casserole dish will do as the name refers to the contents rather than the pot.

lancashire hotpot

500 g/1 lb. braising steak/stewing beef, trimmed of fat

250 g/8 oz. shoulder of lamb, trimmed of fat

2 lamb's kidneys, cleaned and trimmed (optional)

1 tablespoon plain/all-purpose flour

2 tablespoons beef dripping or butter (optional)

1 onion, thinly sliced

1 carrot, cut into chunks

1 bay leaf

300 ml/1¼ cups beef stock or water

½ teaspoon salt

1 teaspoon sugar

¼ teaspoon freshly ground black pepper

1 teaspoon anchovy essence/paste

350 g/12 oz. potatoes, cut into walnut-sized chunks

a flameproof casserole dish

serves 4

Preheat the oven to 180°C (350°F) Gas 4.

Cut the meats into 3-cm/1-inch pieces and sprinkle with the flour. Mix well, then shake off the excess flour through a large sieve/strainer. Arrange the meats in a casserole. If you wish to brown the vegetables, heat the dripping or butter in a frying pan/skillet, add the vegetables and sauté until lightly browned.

Transfer the vegetables, whether browned or not, to the casserole dish. Add the bay leaf, season the boiling stock or water with the salt, sugar, pepper and anchovy essence/paste, then pour over the meats. Cover the casserole dish, bring to the boil on the stovetop, then transfer to the preheated oven and simmer for 1 hour.

Arrange the potatoes, rounded side up, on top of the meats and spoon some of the meat juices over the top to glaze. Cover and return the casserole to the oven for a further hour. Remove the lid to allow the potatoes to become lightly browned and, increasing the heat if necessary, cook for a further 30 minutes.

A sauté is a classic French way to prepare chicken. The chicken is browned first, then simmered and cooking juices reduced slightly just before serving. This one is fast to prepare and it tastes great straight away.

chicken sauté with carrots, leeks, mustard & cream

1 tablespoon extra virgin olive oil

8–10 chicken thighs

300 g/10 oz. carrots, thickly sliced at an angle

300 g/10 oz. leeks, white part only, cut into 2.5-cm/1-inch slices

3 garlic cloves, sliced

250 ml/1 cup dry white wine

a handful of flat leaf parsley, chopped

2 tablespoons double/heavy cream or crème fraîche

1 tablespoon Dijon mustard

sea salt and freshly ground black pepper

a wide, shallow lidded sauté pan

serves 4

Heat the oil in a wide, shallow sauté pan with a lid, large enough to hold the chicken in a single layer. Add the chicken and brown all over, 3–5 minutes a side. Work in batches if necessary. Transfer the browned chicken to a plate, season well with salt.

Add the carrots and leeks to the pan and cook over high heat for 2–3 minutes. Add the garlic and some salt and cook for 1–2 minutes, stirring; do not let the garlic burn. Add the wine and stir, scraping up any bits that stick to the pan.

Return the chicken pieces to the pan and bury under the vegetables. Add the parsley, cover and simmer gently for 20 minutes.

Remove the chicken with tongs. Raise the heat and cook the sauce to reduce slightly, about 8–10 minutes. Stir in the cream and mustard, with salt and pepper to taste. If serving from the pan, return the chicken pieces and serve, or arrange the pieces on plates and spoon the sauce over the top.

This chili is the real thing, made with finely chopped chuck steak instead of mince/ground beef and spiced with several types of chilli/chile, not the ubiquitous powder from the supermarket shelf.

chili with all the trimmings

1 chipotle chilli/chile (dried smoked jalapeño)

4 tablespoons extra virgin olive oil

4 (bell) peppers (1 red, 1 yellow, 1 orange, 1 green), halved, deseeded and chopped

1 large onion

2 celery ribs/stalks, chopped

½–1 green chilli/chile, finely chopped

800 g/2 lbs. chuck steak, cubed

3 garlic cloves

250 ml/1 cup red wine, fresh beef stock or water

¼ teaspoon dried chilli/hot red pepper flakes

2 teaspoons ground cumin

2 teaspoons dried oregano

2 x 400 g/14-oz. cans chopped tomatoes

3 x 400 g/14-oz. cans red kidney beans, drained and rinsed

1 bay leaf

sea salt and freshly ground black pepper

serves 6–8

Put the chipotle in a small bowl and just cover with hot water. Soak for at least 15 minutes, while you prepare the other ingredients.

Heat 2 tablespoons of the oil in a large saucepan. Add the (bell) peppers, onion, celery, green chilli/chile and a good pinch of salt and cook until soft, 5–7 minutes, stirring often. Remove from the pan and set aside. Raise the heat, add the remaining 2 tablespoons of the oil and the meat. Cook, stirring often until browned, 1–2 minutes. Add the garlic and another pinch of salt and cook, stirring constantly for 1 minute. Add the wine and bring to the boil for 1 minute.

Return the peppers to the pan and stir in the chilli/hot red pepper flakes, cumin and oregano. Add the tomatoes, beans, bay leaf and a good pinch of salt and stir well. Remove the chipotle from the soaking liquid, chop finely and stir into the pan, along with the soaking liquid. Cover and simmer gently until the meat is tender, 15–20 minutes. Season to taste.

At this point, the chili is ready, but you should set it aside for at least 2–3 hours before serving to develop the flavours or, ideally, make one day in advance and chill until needed. Serve hot, with all the trimmings in separate bowls.

Note This is best served with all the trimmings: 1–2 ripe avocados, chopped and tossed with lime juice; a bunch of spring onions/scallions, chopped; a bunch of fresh coriander/cilantro, chopped; 8–12 tortillas (at least 2 per person), warmed; sour cream or crème fraîche; freshly grated cheese, such as mild Cheddar or Monterey Jack; lime wedges and Tabasco sauce.

The Italians use a mixture of onions, carrots and celery sautéed in olive oil as the base for many classic soups and casseroles. This holy trinity of veggies is called a *soffritto* and works well here in a hearty stew.

smoky sausage & bean casserole

1 tablespoon light olive oil

12 chipolata sausages

1 garlic clove, chopped

1 leek, thinly sliced

1 carrot, diced

1 celery rib/stalk, diced

1 x 400-g/14-oz. can chopped tomatoes

1 teaspoon Spanish smoked paprika

2 tablespoons maple syrup

2 sprigs of fresh thyme

1 x 400 g/14-oz. can cannellini beans, drained and rinsed

toasted sourdough bread, to serve

serves 4

Heat the oil in a heavy-based saucepan over high heat. Add the sausages in 2 batches and cook them for 4–5 minutes, turning often until cooked and an even brown all over. Remove from the pan and set aside.

Add the garlic, leek, carrot and celery and cook for 5 minutes, stirring often. Add the tomatoes, paprika, maple syrup, thyme, beans and 500 ml/2 cups water and return the sausages to the pan.

Bring to the boil, then reduce the heat to medium and simmer for 40–45 minutes, until the sauce has thickened.

Put a slice of toasted sourdough bread on each serving plate, spoon the casserole over the top and serve.

Variation Try replacing the sausages with 500 g/1 lb. pork neck fillet cut into 2–3-cm/1-inch pieces. Cook the pork in batches for 4–5 minutes each batch, turning often so each piece is evenly browned. Return all the pork to the pan, as you would the sausages, and simmer for 45–50 minutes until the pork is tender.

While lasagne might be considered a safe and even rather dull choice for a party, this version shows why it enjoys such enduring popularity. It will satisfy hardened carnivores and vegetarians alike.

green lasagne with ricotta pesto & mushrooms

250 g/8 oz. fresh spinach lasagne, or 1 package dried green lasagne

Parmesan cheese and butter, to finish

sea salt and freshly ground black pepper

mushroom sauce

25 g/1 cup dried porcini mushrooms

4 tablespoons/¼ cup olive oil

50 g/4 tablespoons unsalted butter

1 kg/2 lbs. fresh wild mushrooms, sliced

1 onion, chopped

4 garlic cloves, chopped

4 tablespoons chopped fresh flat leaf parsley

2–3 sprigs of fresh thyme, chopped

300 ml/1¼ cups chicken or vegetable stock

ricotta pesto

150 g/1 cup fresh green pesto sauce

200 g/1 cup fresh ricotta cheese

an ovenproof baking dish, buttered

serves 6

To make the mushroom sauce, soak the porcini mushrooms in warm water for 20 minutes. Drain, reserving the soaking liquid. Squeeze them gently, then chop coarsely. Heat half the oil and all the butter in a large frying pan/skillet. When foaming, add half the fresh and chopped dried mushrooms and half the onion. Sauté over high heat for 4–5 minutes until tender. Repeat with the remaining mushrooms and onions, then mix the 2 batches in the pan. Stir in the garlic and herbs and cook for 2 minutes. Add the stock and soaking liquid, then boil for 4–5 minutes until the sauce is syrupy. Let cool.

Bring a large saucepan of salted water to the boil and drop in a few lasagne sheets at a time. Fresh pasta is cooked when the water returns to the boil. Lift it out and drain. For dried lasagne, follow the instructions on the package. Stir together the fresh pesto and ricotta in a bowl.

Preheat the oven to 180°C (350°F) Gas 4. Line the prepared ovenproof dish with a layer of lasagne and add a layer of the ricotta and pesto mixture. Add another layer of pasta, then mushroom sauce, then a layer of lasagne. Repeat until all the ingredients have been used, finishing with a lasagne layer. Sprinkle with Parmesan and dot with butter.

Cover with oiled foil and bake in the preheated oven for 20 minutes. Uncover, then bake for a further 20 minutes until golden. Let stand for 10 minutes before serving.

A beautifully balanced dish, perfect for an evening at home with friends. Parsnips and ginger together may be a surprising combination but they are a compelling and interesting variation on traditional mashed potato.

butternut & goats' cheese gratin with parsnip mash

2 kg/4 lbs. butternut squash or pumpkin

4 tablespoons/¼ cup olive oil

50 g/4 tablespoons unsalted butter

350 g/12-oz. canned sweetcorn kernels, drained

½ teaspoon freshly grated nutmeg

2 garlic cloves, crushed

fresh thyme leaves off the stalk

sea salt and freshly ground black pepper

140 g/3 cups fresh breadcrumbs

100 g/4 oz. firm goats'/aged goat cheese, grated

parsnip mash

750 g/1½ lbs. parsnips, coarsely chopped

1 tablespoon sunflower oil

1 teaspoon ground ginger

300 ml/1¼ cups double/heavy cream

sea salt and freshly ground black pepper

2 ovenproof dishes, ideally glass

serves 4

Preheat the oven to 200°C (400°F) Gas 6.

Put the squash in an ovenproof dish with 1 tablespoon of the olive oil, the butter in pieces, corn, nutmeg, garlic, thyme, salt and pepper.

To make the topping, mix the breadcrumbs, goats' cheese and remaining oil in a bowl, then sprinkle over the squash. Cover with foil and bake in the preheated oven for 40 minutes. Remove the foil and cook for a further 15 minutes until golden brown on top.

Meanwhile, make the mash. Put the parsnips on a baking sheet and sprinkle with salt, sunflower oil and ginger. Roast in the preheated oven for about 20 minutes until the parsnips are tender. Transfer to a food processor, add the cream and blend until smooth. Add salt and pepper to taste. Transfer to the second ovenproof glass dish, cover with foil and heat in the oven for 10 minutes. Serve the gratin with the parsnip mash.

The secret of perfect mash is the right potato — a floury variety that fluffs up properly. Older potatoes work better than new and make sure that they are thoroughly cooked or the mash will be lumpy.

perfect mashed potatoes

750 g/1½ lbs. floury potatoes, quartered

55 g/4 tablespoons unsalted butter

75–100 ml/⅓–½ cup whole milk

sea salt and freshly ground black pepper

serves 4

Put the potatoes in a saucepan of salted cold water and bring to the boil. As soon as the water comes to the boil, reduce to a simmer (it's important not to cook the potatoes too quickly) and cook for about 20 minutes. When perfectly done, the point of a sharp knife should glide into the centre.

Drain in a colander, then set over the hot pan to steam and dry out. Tip the potatoes back into the hot pan and crush with a potato masher or pass them through a mouli or ricer into the pan. Melt the butter in the milk. Using a wooden spoon, beat the butter and milk into the mash – an electric hand-mixer sometimes helps here. Season, pile into a warm dish and serve immediately, or alternatively the mash will keep warm in a very cool oven – 120°C (250°F) Gas ½ – for up to 2 hours if covered with buttered foil. Otherwise, cool and reheat gently, beating in extra melted butter and hot milk. If adding herbs, beat in just before serving.

Variation Spring Onion/Scallion and Horseradish Mash: beat in 3 tablespoons chopped spring onions/scallions sautéed in butter and 2 tablespoons creamed horseradish.

It's best not to use waxy potatoes here. You will need tiny little new potatoes to make perfect smashed roast potatoes. The initial blast of a really hot oven is what makes the potatoes so soft and fluffy on the inside.

smashed roast potatoes

16 small new potatoes (such as Nicola or chats)

2 tablespoons light olive oil

1 teaspoon sea salt

a non-stick roasting pan

serves 4

Preheat the oven to 230°C (450°F) Gas 8 and put a non-stick roasting pan in the oven to heat up for 10 minutes.

Put the potatoes in a bowl with 1 tablespoon of the oil and toss to coat in the oil. Put the potatoes in the hot pan and roast in the preheated oven for 20 minutes.

Remove the pan from the oven and turn the potatoes over. Gently press down on each potato with the back of large metal spoon until you hear the potato skin pop.

Drizzle the remaining oil over the potatoes, sprinkle with the sea salt and return to the oven for a further 10 minutes, until the potatoes are crispy and golden brown.

Variation Remove the potatoes from the oven and spoon over a soft French cheese (such as the sweet and nutty L'Edel de Cleron), while the potatoes are still warm. The cheese will melt and transform these humble roasties into a pure indulgence.

Cream and potatoes, mingling in the oven, are all that's needed in this well-loved dish. You can add cheese, but it won't be a true *dauphinois*. Serve on its own, with a mixed green salad, or with a simple roast.

creamy potato gratin

2 kg/4½ lbs. waxy salad-style potatoes, cut into half if large

2 litres/quarts whole milk

1 fresh bay leaf

30 g/2 tablespoons unsalted butter

550 ml/2 cups whipping cream

a pinch of grated nutmeg

coarse sea salt

a baking dish

serves 4–6

Preheat the oven to 180°C (350°F) Gas 4.

Put the potatoes in a large saucepan with the milk and bay leaf. Bring to the boil, then lower the heat, add a pinch of salt and simmer gently until part-cooked, 5–10 minutes.

Drain the potatoes. When cool enough to handle (but still hot), slice into rounds about 3-mm/¼-inch thick.

Spread the butter in the bottom of a baking dish. Arrange half the potato slices in the dish and sprinkle with salt. Put the remaining potato on top and sprinkle with more salt. Pour in the cream and sprinkle with the grated nutmeg.

Bake in the preheated oven for about 45 minutes, until golden and the cream is almost absorbed, but not completely. Serve hot as a side dish with meat or fish.

A regular accompaniment on the *plat du jour* circuit, this recipe goes well with pork. The secret of delicious cauliflower is to blanch it first; parboil it with a bay leaf and the unpleasant cabbage aroma disappears.

cauliflower gratin

1 large cauliflower, separated into large florets

1 fresh bay leaf

500 ml/2 cups double/heavy cream

2 teaspoons Dijon mustard

1 egg

160 g/1½ cups finely grated Comté or Emmenthal cheese*

coarse sea salt

a baking dish, greased

serves 4–6

Preheat the oven to 200°C (400°F) Gas 6.

Bring a large saucepan of water to the boil, add the bay leaf, salt generously, then add the cauliflower. Cook until still slightly firm, about 10 minutes. Drain and set aside.

Put the cream in a saucepan and bring to the boil. Boil for 10 minutes, then stir in the mustard, the egg and 1 teaspoon salt.

Divide the cauliflower into smaller florets, then stir into the cream sauce. Transfer to the prepared baking dish and sprinkle the cheese over the top in an even layer. Bake in the preheated oven until golden, about 40–45 minutes. Serve hot as a side dish or a light supper.

*Note Like the Swiss cheese Gruyère, Comté is a mountain cheese – from the Franche-Comté region to be precise – but the similarity stops there. Comté's distinct flavour comes from the milk used in the making, so the flavour varies with the seasons. Use Emmenthal if it is unavailable.

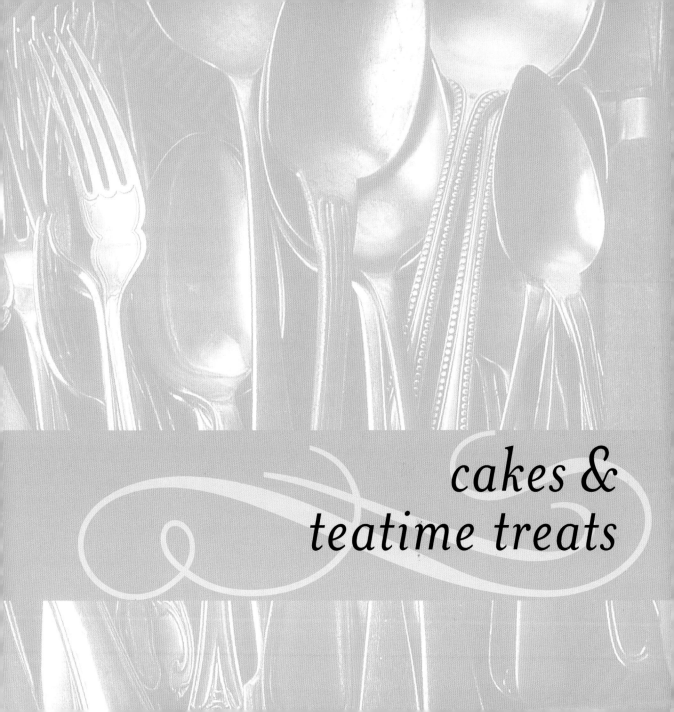

cakes &
teatime treats

This is a great recipe – a smooth, dense cake given a light and creamy crumb by using buttermilk. It can be made in a conventional round cake pan or baked in a rectangular pan and cut into squares to serve.

strawberry buttermilk cake

250 g/2 cups self-raising/rising flour

225 g/1 cup plus 2 tablespoons caster/superfine sugar

125 g/1 stick unsalted butter, softened

2 eggs

225 g/1 cup buttermilk

375 g/12 oz. strawberries, hulled, large ones halved

vanilla custard or double/heavy cream, to serve

crumble topping

40 g/5 tablespoons plain/ all-purpose flour

50 g/½ stick unsalted butter, chilled and cubed

95 g/½ cup packed soft brown sugar

a cake pan, 24-cm/8-inches square, greased and lined

serves 6–8

Preheat the oven to 180°C (350°F) Gas 4.

Put the flour and sugar in a bowl and mix. Put the butter, eggs and buttermilk in a food processor and process until smooth and combined. With the motor running, add the flour and sugar and process until well mixed. Scrape down the sides of the bowl to evenly incorporate all the ingredients. Transfer the mixture to a bowl and stir in the strawberries. Spoon the batter into the prepared cake pan.

To make the crumble topping, put the flour and butter in a bowl and, using the tips of your fingers, rub the butter into the flour until the mixture resembles coarse breadcrumbs. Stir in the sugar.

Evenly sprinkle the topping mixture over the cake and bake in the preheated oven for 50 minutes, until golden brown on top.

Let cool before cutting into slices or squares and serving with vanilla custard or a dollop of double/heavy cream.

This cake uses a cream-cheese batter. Vary it with some additions: mini marshmallows thrown in with the chocolate chips, coarsely chopped almonds and/or hazelnuts, or a heaped teaspoon of ground cinnamon.

chocolate chip cake

100 g/3½ oz. best-quality plain/bittersweet chocolate

100 g/7 tablespoons unsalted butter

200 g/1 cup caster/superfine sugar

200 g/8 oz. cream cheese

2 eggs

200 g/1½ cups plain/all-purpose flour

1½ teaspoons baking powder

a pinch of fine sea salt

100 g/3½ oz. plain/bittersweet chocolate chips

a loaf pan, 27.5 x 8.5 cm/ 9 x 5 inches, greased and lined

serves 6–8

Preheat the oven to 190°C (375°F) Gas 5.

Put the chocolate and butter in a microwave-proof bowl and microwave on 'medium' for 1 minute. Stir and repeat until the chocolate has almost completely melted; stop just short and let the rest melt from the residual heat. Set aside to cool.

Put the sugar and cream cheese in the bowl of an electric mixer and beat on high until well blended. Add the eggs and chocolate mixture and continue beating until well mixed.

Put the flour, baking powder and salt in another bowl and mix well. Add to the cream-cheese mixture, with the beaters on low, until just blended. Fold in the chocolate chips. Pour into the prepared loaf pan.

Bake in the preheated oven for about 40–45 minutes until just brown around the edges and a skewer comes out almost clean when inserted in the middle, .

This elegant, mile-high, three-layer sponge cake is feather-light but full of rich flavours. It is very delicate, and cuts best the next day. Store at room temperature overnight in an airtight container.

maple syrup pecan cake

350 g/3 sticks unsalted butter, at room temperature

280 g/1½ cups caster/superfine sugar

4 large eggs, lightly beaten

3 tablespoons pure maple syrup

120 g/1¼ cups pecan nuts, finely chopped (in a food processor), but not ground

350 g/2⅓ cups self-raising/rising flour, sieved

a pinch of salt

icing/frosting

225 ml/1 cup pure maple syrup

2 large egg whites

pecan halves, to decorate

3 sandwich pans, 20-cm/8-inch diameter, greased and base-lined

serves 6–8

Preheat the oven to 180°C (350°F) Gas 4.

Using an electric mixer, beat the butter until lighter in colour, then add the sugar, a spoonful at a time, while still beating. Scrape down the sides of the bowl, then beat until the mixture is very light and fluffy. Beat in the eggs a spoonful at a time, then gradually beat in the maple syrup. Add the pecans, flour and salt to the bowl and, using a large metal spoon or rubber spatula, gently fold into the mixture.

Divide the mixture between the 3 prepared pans and spread evenly. Bake in the preheated oven for 25–30 minutes, until the cakes are golden and springy to the touch. Let cool for a minute, then run a round-bladed knife around the inside edge of the pans to loosen the sponges and carefully turn out onto a wire rack to cool completely.

Meanwhile, to make the icing/frosting, heat the maple syrup in a medium, heavy pan and let boil gently for about 5 minutes, watching to check it does not bubble up and boil over. While the syrup is heating, whisk the egg whites until stiff peaks form. Pour the hot syrup onto the egg whites in a thin stream while still whisking constantly. Keep whisking for a further 1 minute or until the icing/frosting is very thick and fluffy.

When the cakes are completely cold, use the icing/frosting to layer them. Spread about one-sixth of the mixture on top of one cake. Gently set a second cake on top and spread with another one-sixth of the icing/frosting. Top with the last cake, then coat the top and sides with the rest of the icing/frosting. Decorate with pecan halves.

There is something almost virtuous about a cake that is baked with vegetables in it. In fact, this is also known as 'passion cake' and makes a truly scrumptious teatime treat.

carrot cake

4 eggs, separated

240 g/1 cup packed soft brown sugar

zest and juice of 1 unwaxed orange

240 g/1²⁄₃ cups ground walnuts

1 teaspoon ground cinnamon

250 g/1½ cups carrot, grated

100 g/¾ cup wholemeal/whole-wheat flour

1 teaspoon baking powder

frosting

200 g/8 oz. cream cheese

100 g/²⁄₃ cup icing/confectioners' sugar

zest and juice of 1 small unwaxed orange

a loose-bottomed cake pan, 20-cm/8-inches square, greased

serves 6–8

Preheat the oven to 180°C (350°F) Gas 4.

Put the egg yolks and sugar in a bowl and whisk until thick and creamy. Add all the remaining ingredients, except the egg whites, and fold carefully until the mixture is smooth.

Whisk the egg whites until stiff, then fold into the cake mixture. Pour into the prepared cake pan and bake in the centre of the oven for 1 hour. When done, cool in the pan for 5 minutes, then turn out and cool completely on a wire rack.

To make the frosting, cream the cheese and icing/confectioners' sugar together. Add a little orange zest and juice to flavour. Spread over the top of the cold cake using a palette knife dipped in hot water. Sprinkle with the remaining orange zest.

With a gooey chocolate and hazelnut centre, these luscious cakes are a real treat. Stirring chocolate and hazelnut spread into the creamy frosting gives it a wonderfully nutty taste.

gooey chocolate & hazelnut cupcakes

75 g/2½ oz. dark/bittersweet chocolate, chopped

100 g/6½ tablespoons unsalted butter, at room temperature

100 g/½ cup caster/superfine sugar

2 eggs

25 g/3 tablespoons blanched hazelnuts, ground

100 g/¾ cup self-raising/rising flour

100 g/½ cup chocolate and hazelnut spread, such as Nutella

to decorate

100 g/3½ oz. dark/bittersweet chocolate, finely chopped

100 ml/½ cup double/heavy cream

2 tablespoons chocolate and hazelnut spread, such as Nutella

about 25 g/3 tablespoons blanched hazelnuts, toasted and cut into large pieces

a 12-hole cupcake pan, lined with paper liners

makes 12 cupcakes

Preheat the oven to 180°C (350°F) Gas 4.

Put the chocolate in a heatproof bowl set over a pan of gently simmering water. Do not let the bowl touch the water. Leave until almost melted. Remove from the heat and leave to cool.

Beat the butter and sugar together in a bowl until pale and fluffy, then beat in the eggs, one at a time. Stir in the hazelnuts, then sift the flour into the mixture and fold in. Stir in the melted chocolate.

Drop ½ a heaped tablespoonful of the mixture into each paper case, then flatten and make an indentation in the centre using the back of a teaspoon. Drop a generous dollop of chocolate spread into the centre of each one, then top with the remaining cake mixture. Bake in the preheated oven for about 18 minutes until risen and the tops spring back when gently pressed. Transfer to a wire rack to cool.

To decorate, put the chocolate in a heatproof bowl. Heat the cream in a saucepan until almost boiling, then pour over the chocolate and leave to stand for about 5 minutes. Stir until smooth and creamy, then leave to cool for about 30 minutes until thick and glossy.

Spread the frosting over the cakes and arrange a cluster of nuts in the centre of each one.

Inspired by the classic banoffee pie, these creamy cakes are to die for. The tender, moist banana cakes are packed with nuggets of chewy toffee, then topped with whipped cream, dulce de leche and fresh banana.

banoffee cupcakes

60 g/4 tablespoons butter, at room temperature

70 g/⅓ cup packed soft brown sugar

1 egg

1 ripe banana, mashed

115 g/1 cup self-raising/rising flour

50 g/4 chewy toffees/caramels, chopped

to decorate

180 ml/⅔ cup double/heavy cream, whipped

3–4 tablespoons *dulce de leche**

1 banana, sliced

a 12-hole cupcake pan, lined with 10 paper liners

makes 10 cupcakes

Preheat the oven to 180°C (350°F) Gas 4.

Beat the butter and sugar together in a bowl until creamy, then beat in the egg, a little at a time. Fold in the mashed banana, then sift the flour into the mixture and fold in, followed by the toffees/caramels.

Spoon the mixture into the paper liners and bake for about 15 minutes until risen and a skewer inserted in the centre comes out clean. Transfer to a wire rack to cool.

To decorate, swirl the cream over each of the cakes, then drizzle with a spoonful of *dulce de leche* and top with slices of banana.

*Note Dulce de leche is a sweet, gooey caramel sauce from Spain, which is available from larger supermarkets. If you can't find it, you can make it yourself. Put a sealed can of condensed milk in a saucepan, pour over boiling water to cover and boil for 3 hours, adding more water as necessary so that the can is always covered. Remove from the pan and leave to cool completely before opening using a can opener. Stir well to make a smooth sauce before spooning over the cakes.

The combination of chocolate, marshmallows and nuts in these sweet and sticky cakes is a taste of pure indulgence. Only add the toppings if you've got a really sweet tooth; if not the chocolate will be enough.

rocky road cupcakes

115 g/1 stick butter, at room temperature

100 g/½ cup granulated sugar

2 eggs

115 g/1 cup self-raising/rising flour

3 tablespoons unsweetened cocoa powder

3 tablespoons milk

25 g/1 oz. white chocolate chips

50 g/1 cup mini marshmallows

25 g/2 tablespoons flaked/slivered almonds or brazil nuts

to decorate

100 g/3½ oz. dark/bittersweet chocolate, chopped

100 ml/½ cup double/heavy cream

25 g/3 tablespoons each flaked/slivered almonds or brazil nuts, white chocolate chips and mini marshmallows (optional)

a 12-hole muffin pan, lined with paper liners

makes 12 cupcakes

Preheat the oven to 180°C (350°F) Gas 4.

Beat the butter and sugar together in a bowl until pale and fluffy, then beat in the eggs, one at a time. Sift the flour and cocoa into the mixture and fold in. Stir in the milk, followed by the chocolate chips, marshmallows and nuts.

Spoon the mixture into the paper liners and bake for about 18 minutes until risen and the tops spring back when lightly pressed. Transfer to a wire rack to cool.

Meanwhile prepare the decoration. Put the chocolate in a heatproof bowl. Heat the cream in a saucepan until almost boiling, then pour over the chocolate and leave to stand for about 5 minutes. Stir until smooth and creamy, then leave to cool for about 30 minutes until thick and glossy.

Spread the chocolate mixture over the cakes and sprinkle with nuts, chocolate chips and marshmallows, if liked.

Whether you are hosting a sophisticated coffee morning or wanting to top off an elegant dinner party, this delicious pudding cake will provide the ideal accompaniment to freshly brewed coffee.

sticky toffee pudding cake

150 g/¼ cup dried dates, chopped

1 teaspoon bicarbonate of/ baking soda

225 ml/1 cup moderately strong hot black coffee (e.g. from a cafetière)

150 g/1 cup plus 2 tablespoons plain/ all-purpose flour

50 g/3 tablespoons butter, chilled and cubed

50 g/⅓ cup walnuts, finely chopped

200 g/1 cup golden caster/superfine sugar

1 teaspoon baking powder

½ teaspoon fine sea salt

1 large egg

½ teaspoon vanilla extract

for the topping

50 g/⅓ cup walnuts, finely chopped

1 teaspoon golden caster/superfine sugar

25 g/2 tablespoons unsalted butter

4 tablespoons/¼ cup soft light brown sugar

4 tablespoons whipping cream

a non-stick cake pan, 30.5 x 20.5 cm/ 12 x 8 inches, lightly greased

Preheat the oven to 180°C (350°F) Gas 4.

Put the chopped dates in a bowl, add the bicarbonate of/baking soda and pour over the hot coffee. Put the flour in another bowl, tip in the cubed butter and cut and rub it in until it resembles coarse breadcrumbs.

Add the chopped walnuts to the flour mixture with the sugar, baking powder and salt. Beat the egg with the vanilla extract and add to the date mixture, then tip the date mixture into the dry ingredients and beat well. Turn the mixture into the prepared pan and bake in the preheated oven for about 35–40 minutes or until well risen and firm to the touch. Remove from the oven and let cool for 10 minutes while you make the topping.

Heat the walnuts in a saucepan with the caster/superfine sugar, shaking them occasionally until they are lightly toasted. Combine the butter in a small saucepan with the brown sugar and cream. Heat over low heat, stirring until the sugar has dissolved, then bring to the boil. Pour evenly over the cake, smoothing over the topping with a knife, then scatter the toasted walnuts on top.

When the cake is completely cool, cut it into squares and carefully remove from the pan using a cake slice or palette knife.

This wonderfully fudgy cake is perfect for a birthday or any other party. Cool completely before you cut it. Like all chocolate cakes, it is best made the day before you plan to eat it. Store in an airtight container.

best-ever chocolate cake

100 g/½ cup caster/superfine sugar

115 g/1 stick unsalted butter, at room temperature, plus extra for greasing

½ teaspoon vanilla extract

2 large eggs, at room temperature

230 ml/1 cup sour cream, at room temperature

250 g/1¾ cups plain/all-purpose flour

40 g/½ cup unsweetened cocoa powder

1 teaspoon baking powder

1 teaspoon bicarbonate of/baking soda

a pinch of salt

chocolate frosting/icing

175 g/6 oz. best-quality milk chocolate

90 g/3½ oz. plain/semi-sweet chocolate

230 ml/1 cup sour cream

2 sandwich cake pans, 20-cm/8-inches diameter, greased and base-lined

serves 8–10

Preheat the oven to 180°C (350°F) Gas 4.

Put the sugar, butter and vanilla in a large bowl. Break the eggs into the bowl, then add the sour cream. Sift flour, cocoa powder, baking powder, bicarbonate of/baking soda and salt into the bowl. Using a wooden spoon or electric hand mixer on slow speed, beat the mixture for about 1 minute until smooth.

Spoon the mixture into the prepared pans so they are evenly filled, then spread the mixture so it is smooth. Bake in the preheated oven for 20 minutes, then cool on a wire rack.

Meanwhile, make the frosting/icing. Break up the chocolate and put it into a heatproof bowl. Set the bowl over the pan of hot water and let the chocolate melt, stirring. When the chocolate has melted, remove the bowl from the pan and let the chocolate cool for 5 minutes. Gently stir in the sour cream to make a smooth, thick frosting/icing.

When the cakes have cooled, set one of the cakes on a serving plate. Spread about one-third of the frosting/icing over the cake, then set the second cake gently on top of the first. Spread the rest of the frosting/icing on the top and sides of the cake to cover it completely.

For the best results, use a good-quality peanut butter with no added sugar. The crunchy coating is made by rolling the cookie mixture in roasted (but unsalted) peanuts before baking.

extra-crunchy peanut butter cookies

115 g/1 stick unsalted butter, softened

125 g/½ cup crunchy peanut butter

140 g/¾ cup packed light muscovado/ light brown sugar

1 large egg, lightly beaten

½ teaspoon vanilla extract

225 g/1½ cups self-raising/rising flour

200 g/1⅓ cups roasted unsalted peanut halves

makes 20

Preheat the oven to 180°C (350°F) Gas 4.

Put the soft butter, peanut butter, sugar, beaten egg, vanilla and flour in a large bowl. Mix well with a wooden spoon. When thoroughly combined, take walnut-sized portions of the dough (about a tablespoon) and roll into balls with your hands. Put the peanut halves in a shallow dish, then roll the dough in the nuts. Arrange the balls well apart on to several greased baking sheets, then gently flatten slightly with your fingers.

Bake in the preheated oven for 12–15 minutes until light golden brown. Let cool on the baking sheets for a couple of minutes to firm up, then transfer to a wire rack to cool completely.

Store in an airtight container and eat within 5 days or freeze for up to a month.

Always popular and hard to beat! We've adapted the classic recipe so that it uses less sugar and more nuts. Use plain/semi-sweet chocolate broken up into chunks or a bag of chocolate chips.

classic choc chip cookies

175 g/1⅓ cups self-raising/rising flour

a pinch of salt

a good pinch of bicarbonate of/baking soda

115 g/1 stick unsalted butter, very soft

60 g/⅓ cup caster/superfine sugar

60 g/⅓ cup packed light muscovado/ light brown sugar

½ teaspoon vanilla extract

1 large egg, lightly beaten

175 g/1 cup plain/semi-sweet chocolate chunks or chips

75 g/¾ cup walnut or pecan pieces

makes 24

Preheat the oven to 190°C (375°F) Gas 5.

Put all the ingredients in a large bowl and mix thoroughly with a wooden spoon.

Drop heaped teaspoons of the mixture onto several greased baking sheets, spacing them well apart.

Bake in the preheated oven for 8–10 minutes until lightly coloured and just firm. Let cool on the baking sheets for a minute, then transfer to a wire rack to cool completely.

Store in an airtight container and eat within 5 days or freeze for up to a month.

Homemade cookies never fail to score points from young and old alike. This very quick rich recipe, made using plain/semi-sweet chocolate and a food processor, is really good served with ice cream.

chocolate fudge cookies

75 g/⅓ cup caster/superfine sugar

75 g/½ cup firmly packed light muscovado/light brown sugar

140 g/5 oz. good-quality plain/semi-sweet chocolate, broken up

110 g/1 stick unsalted butter, chilled and cubed

150 g/1¼ cups plain/all-purpose flour

¼ teaspoon baking powder

1 large egg, lightly beaten

makes about 20

Preheat the oven to 180°C (350°F) Gas 4.

Put both the sugars in a food processor. Add the pieces of chocolate, then process until the mixture has a sandy texture.

Add the pieces of butter, flour, baking powder and egg and process until the mixture comes together to make a firm dough. Carefully remove from the machine.

Lightly flour your hands and roll the dough into about 20 walnut-sized balls. Arrange them, spaced well apart, on several greased baking sheets. Bake in the preheated oven for 12–15 minutes until firm. Let cool on the baking sheets for 2 minutes, then transfer to wire racks to cool completely.

Store in an airtight container and eat within 5 days or freeze for up to a month.

Variation Remove the dough from the processor and work in 75 g/½ cup pecan pieces, then shape and bake the cookies as above.

These to-die-for brownies are incredibly rich in chocolate and not too sweet. This is a very useful recipe when you need a flour-free dessert or cake. Undercooking is vital to avoid a crumbly texture.

flourless-yet-fudgy brownies

300 g/10 oz. good-quality plain/
bittersweet chocolate

150 g/1⅓ sticks unsalted butter, diced

50 g/½ cup unsweetened cocoa
powder, sifted

4 large eggs

200 g/1 cup caster/superfine sugar

100 g/1 cup walnut or pecan pieces

icing/confectioners' sugar, for dusting

*a brownie pan, 20.5 x 25.5 cm/
8 x 10 inches, greased and base-lined*

makes 12

Preheat the oven to 180°C (350°F) Gas 4.

Break up the chocolate and put it in a heatproof bowl with the butter. Set the bowl over a pan of steaming hot water and melt gently, stirring frequently. Remove the bowl from the pan and stir in the cocoa. Set aside until needed.

Put the eggs into a mixing bowl and beat well with a whisk or an electric mixer. Add the sugar and whisk thoroughly until very light and frothy and doubled in volume.

Using a large metal spoon, carefully fold in the chocolate mixture followed by the nuts. Transfer the mixture to the prepared pan and spread evenly.

Bake in the preheated oven for about 25–30 minutes until the top of the brownie is just firm to the touch but the centre is still slightly soft.

Leave to cool for 10 minutes before carefully removing from the pan. Dust with icing/confectioners' sugar before cutting into 12 pieces. Once cool, store in an airtight container and eat within 4 days. Serve warm or at room temperature with a generous spoonful of sour cream or crème fraîche.

Blondies are like brownies but flavoured with sugar instead of chocolate. This blondie doesn't contain nuts but you could replace the chocolate with 100 g/ 3–4 oz. of walnut halves or chopped Brazil nuts.

butterscotch blondies

115 g/1 stick unsalted butter

230 g/1⅓ cups firmly packed light muscovado/light brown sugar

2 large eggs, lightly beaten

½ teaspoon vanilla extract

180 g/1⅓ cups plain/all-purpose flour

½ teaspoon baking powder

100 g/3½ oz. good-quality plain/ bittersweet chocolate, chopped or 100 g/⅔ cup plain choc chips

a brownie pan, 20.5 x 25.5 cm/ 8 x 10 inches, greased and base-lined

makes 20

Preheat the oven to 180°C (350°F) Gas 4.

Put the butter in a medium-sized saucepan and melt gently over low heat. Remove the pan from the heat and stir in the sugar with a wooden spoon. Gradually stir in the eggs, then the vanilla and beat for a minute.

Sift the flour and baking powder onto the mixture and stir in. Add the chocolate pieces or choc chips (or nuts if using) and stir until thoroughly combined. Transfer the mixture to the prepared pan and spread evenly.

Bake in the preheated oven for about 25 minutes until light golden brown and a skewer inserted halfway between the sides and the centre comes out just clean.

Leave to cool before removing from the pan and cutting into 20 pieces. Store in an airtight container and eat within 5 days.

Chocolate-hazelnut spread is wonderful scooped out of the jar and devoured by the spoonful. But when warmed up between two pieces of brioche with some banana, it becomes something sublime!

chocolate–hazelnut bananas on brioche

4 thick slices of brioche bread

4 tablespoons chocolate-hazelnut spread, such as Nutella

1 small banana, thinly sliced

vegetable oil, for brushing

a panini press

serves 2

Preheat a panini press.

Spread 2 slices of the brioche with the chocolate-hazelnut spread. Place the banana slices on top. Close the sandwiches with the second slice of brioche.

Brush both sides of the sandwich with a little oil, then toast in the preheated panini press for 2 minutes, or according to the manufacturer's instructions. The bread should be golden brown and the chocolate-banana filling warmed through.

Variation As an alternative, try replacing the chocolate-hazelnut spread with a good-quality wholenut peanut butter.

Buttery, sticky, gooey, tangy bananas — yum! Just be careful because the bananas are hot when they come out of the pan. The dense Jewish bread challah makes the perfect base, as will any good-quality white bread.

sticky sautéed bananas on toast

4 tablespoons butter, plus extra for spreading

3 perfectly ripe bananas, sliced

2 tablespoons brown sugar

1 tablespoon brandy

½ lime

2 thick slices of challah or other white bread

double/heavy cream or vanilla ice cream, to serve

serves 2

Melt the butter in a non-stick frying pan/skillet until sizzling, then add the bananas and sauté for about 2 minutes. Turn them over, sprinkle with the sugar, and continue cooking for a further 2–3 minutes, gently nudging the bananas around the pan, but taking care not to break them up.

Add the brandy and cook for 1 minute more until the bananas are soft and tender, letting the juices bubble. Remove the pan from the heat, squeeze over the lime juice, and shake the bananas to mix.

Meanwhile, lightly toast the bread on both sides, add the bananas, and top with cream or a generous scoop of vanilla ice cream.

Using coconut milk instead of ordinary milk adds an exotic twist to this indulgent dish. For a slightly healthier version, serve with Greek yoghurt instead of cream.

panettone french toast with coconut milk

½ vanilla pod/bean

150 ml/⅔ cup canned coconut milk

2 eggs, lightly beaten

25 g/2 tablespoons caster/superfine sugar

¼ teaspoon ground cardamom (optional)

50 g/4 tablespoons butter

8 slices of panettone or other sweet bread

to serve

icing/confectioners' sugar, for dusting

a punnet/basket of blueberries

clotted or whipped cream

serves 4

Split the vanilla pod/bean in half lengthways and scrape out the seeds. Put the coconut milk, eggs, sugar, vanilla seeds and cardamom, if using, in a bowl and beat well. Pour the mixture into a shallow dish.

Heat half the butter in a large frying pan/skillet. Dip 2 slices of panettone into the egg mixture, then fry until golden on both sides. Repeat with the remaining slices.

Serve dusted with icing/confectioners' sugar and topped with the blueberries and cream.

desserts

Rolling this rustic and crumbly pastry (which is deliciously spicy) and filling it with lemon-infused apples is a very organic process you will want to enjoy again and again, particularly once you have tasted it.

dusky apple pie

8 tart green apples (such as Granny Smith), peeled, cored and thinly sliced

2 teaspoons freshly squeezed lemon juice

2 thin strips of lemon zest

55 g/¼ cup caster/granulated sugar

250 g/2 cups self-raising/rising flour

185 g/¾ cup packed brown sugar

1 tablespoon ground cinnamon

1 tablespoon ground ginger

125 g/1 stick cold butter, cubed

1 egg, lightly beaten

vanilla ice cream, to serve (optional)

a loose-based, fluted, 20 cm/8-inch diameter tart pan, lightly greased

serves 8–10

Put the apple slices in a saucepan with the lemon juice, lemon zest and caster/granulated sugar. Cover and cook over low heat for 15–20 minutes, turning the apples often so they soften and cook evenly. Set aside and let cool.

To make the pastry, put the flour, brown sugar and spices in a food processor and process for a few seconds to combine. With the motor running, add the butter several cubes at a time. Add the egg and 1–2 tablespoons cold water and process until combined. The dough will look dry and crumbly. Transfer to a bowl and knead to form a ball. Wrap the ball in clingfilm/plastic wrap and refrigerate for 30 minutes.

Preheat the oven to 180°C (350°F) Gas 4. Put a baking sheet in the oven to heat up.

Cut the dough into two portions, with one slightly larger than the other. Roll the larger piece of dough between two sheets of wax paper and use it to line the bottom and sides of the prepared tart pan. (Take care when handling the pastry as it will be quite crumbly.) Trim the edge of the pastry to fit the pan.

Spoon the apples on top of the pastry base. Roll the remaining pastry to a circle large enough to cover the base and place on top of the pie, trimming the edges to fit. Use a small sharp knife to make several slits in the pastry. Put the pie on the hot baking sheet and bake in the preheated oven for 50–55 minutes, until the pastry is dark brown. Remove the pie from the oven and leave it to rest for 15–20 minutes before cutting into wedges and serving with vanilla ice cream on the side.

Baking a brownie mixture in a crisp pastry case means you can make the brownie filling very soft, sticky and nutty. This pie is particularly good served warm with ice cream or cream, but it will keep for 5 days.

brownie fudge pie

pastry

175 g/1⅓ cups plain/all-purpose flour

a pinch of salt

115 g/1 stick unsalted butter, chilled and cubed

2–3 tablespoons ice cold water

filling

3 large eggs

150 g/1 cup firm packed light muscovado/light brown sugar

150 g/1 cup firm packed dark muscovado/dark brown sugar

½ teaspoon vanilla extract

175 g/1½ sticks unsalted butter, melted

50 g/⅓ cup plus 1 tablespoon plain/all-purpose flour

50 g/½ cup unsweetened cocoa powder

150 g/1½ cups pecan halves or pieces

a 23-cm/9-inch loose-based flan pan

serves 10

To make the pastry in a food processor put the flour, salt and cubed butter in the bowl and process until the mixture resembles fine crumbs. With the machine running add just enough water through the feed tube to make a slightly firm dough. Alternatively, make the pastry by hand: put the flour, salt and butter into a mixing bowl. Rub the pieces of butter into the flour with your fingertips until the mixture looks like fine crumbs. With a round-bladed knife stir in just enough water to bring the mixture together to make a slightly firm dough. Wrap and chill for 15 minutes.

Roll out the dough on a lightly floured work surface to a circle about 28 cm/11 inches across and use to line the flan pan. Prick the bottom of the pastry case all over with a fork, then chill for 15 minutes.

Preheat the oven to 180°C (350°F) Gas 4. Line the pastry case with wax paper, weigh down with baking beans or rice and bake blind in the preheated oven for 12–15 minutes until lightly golden and just firm. Carefully remove the paper and beans and bake for a further 5 minutes or until the base is crisp and lightly golden. Remove from the oven and leave to cool while making the filling.

Break the eggs into the bowl of an electric mixer. Whisk until frothy then add the sugar and whisk until very thick and mousse-like. Add the vanilla and whisk again to combine. Whisk in the melted butter. Remove the bowl from the mixer and sift the flour and cocoa onto the mixture. Fold in with a large metal spoon. When there are no streaks of flour left, gently stir in the pecans. Transfer the mixture to the pastry case and spread evenly. Bake in the preheated oven for about 30 minutes or until firm to the touch. Remove from the oven and cool slightly before removing from the pan.

While this pie might seem like a lot of effort, it will all seem worth it at your first bite. The lemon filling should be hot when topping with the meringue, as it steams the egg whites and ensures that they stay firm.

lemon meringue pie

1 recipe Basic Pie Case
(page 234)

filling

200 g/1 scant cup caster/granulated sugar

30 g/¼ cup cornflour/cornstarch

a pinch of salt

5 egg yolks

125 ml/½ cup freshly squeezed lemon juice

1 tablespoon grated lemon zest

3 tablespoons unsalted butter

1 teaspoon vanilla extract

meringue

1 tablespoon cornflour/cornstarch

5 egg whites

a pinch of salt

¼ teaspoon cream of tartar

100 g/½ cup caster/superfine sugar

serves 8

To make the filling, combine 350 ml/1½ cups cold water, the sugar, cornflour/cornstarch and salt in a saucepan. Over medium/high heat, bring the mixture to the boil, whisking constantly. Remove from the heat. In a medium bowl, whisk the egg yolks. Pour about ½ cup of the sugar mixture into the egg yolks and whisk well. Pour the yolk mixture back into the saucepan. Bring the mixture to the boil over medium/high heat, whisking constantly. Boil for 1 minute, then remove from the heat. Whisk in the lemon juice, zest and butter and finally the vanilla extract. Set aside while you make the meringue topping.

Preheat the grill/broiler and make the meringue. Heat the cornflour/cornstarch and 75 ml/⅓ cup water in a small saucepan. Bring to the boil over medium/high heat, stirring constantly. Boil for 30 seconds and remove from the heat. In a large bowl, beat the egg whites with an electric whisk on a low speed until they are frothy. Add the salt and cream of tartar, turn the speed up to medium/high and beat until the whites form soft peaks. Add the sugar 1 spoonful at a time until the meringue is very glossy. Add a little of the meringue to the cornflour/cornstarch mixture and stir. Pour this slowly back into the meringue and whisk on high speed until stiff peaks form.

Reheat the lemon mixture until hot. Pour this into the pie case. Gently spoon the meringue over the surface, making sure that it adheres to the crust and is well sealed. Use the back of a spoon to make decorative peaks and swirls on top. Put on a rack 10–15 cm/4–6 inches under a very hot grill/broiler for about 5 minutes, or until browned. Leave to cool completely on a rack then refrigerate until ready to serve. Eat on the same day of preparation.

Walnuts are heavenly packed in a soft, sticky tart, which is superb with the quick fudge ice cream. In fact, the plain vanilla ice cream marbled with fudge toffee is a treat to enjoy just on its own.

walnut tart with quick fudge ice cream

1 recipe Sweet Shortcrust Pastry (page 235)

walnut filling

125 g/1¼ sticks unsalted butter, softened

125 g/½ cup plus 2 tablespoons light brown sugar

3 large eggs

grated zest and juice of 1 small orange

175 g/¾ cup golden/light corn syrup

225 g/8 oz. shelled walnut pieces

a pinch of salt

quick fudge/caramel ice cream

150 g/6 oz. chewy toffees/caramels

100 g/½ cup double/heavy cream

600 ml/1 pint best-quality vanilla ice cream, softened

a fluted tart pan, 23-cm/9-inches diameter

serves 6

Bring the pastry to room temperature. Preheat the oven to 190°C (375°F) Gas 5.

Roll out the pastry on a lightly floured work surface and use to line the tart pan. Prick the base, chill or freeze for 15 minutes, then bake blind (follow the method given in the recipe on page 192). Leave to cool. Lower the oven to 180°C (350°F) Gas 4.

To make the filling, put the butter and sugar into a bowl and cream until light and fluffy. Gradually beat in the eggs, one at a time. Beat the orange zest and juice into the butter and egg mixture. Heat the syrup in a small saucepan until runny, but not very hot. Stir into the butter mixture, then stir in the walnuts and salt.

Pour into the pastry case and bake for 45 minutes until lightly browned and risen. The tart will sink a little on cooling.

While the tart is cooling, make the ice cream. Put the toffees/caramels and double/heavy cream into a small saucepan and stir over medium heat to melt. Leave to cool slightly and stir quickly into the ice cream so that it looks marbled. Put the ice cream back in the freezer until ready to serve.

Serve the tart at room temperature with scoops of the ice cream.

Bread and butter pudding is a traditional British favourite, which was revived a few years ago. This version bakes them in individual dishes, and they will cook in under 20 minutes.

bread & butter puddings

300 ml/1¼ cups milk

300 ml/1¼ cups double/heavy cream

½ teaspoon vanilla extract

4 tablespoons caster/superfine sugar

3 eggs

6 tea cakes/slices of brioche or hot cross buns, halved

50 g/⅓ cup sultanas/golden raisins

1 whole nutmeg

6 x 200-ml/1- cup ramekins or ovenproof individual serving dishes, buttered

serves 6

Preheat the oven to 180°C (350°F) Gas 4.

Put the milk, cream, vanilla extract and 3 tablespoons of the sugar into a saucepan and heat until the sugar dissolves.

Put the eggs into a bowl, whisk them well, then stir in 2–3 tablespoons of the hot milk mixture to warm the eggs. Stir in the remainder of the hot milk.

Lightly toast the tea cakes/brioche or hot cross buns and cut into quarters. Divide them between the prepared ramekins and sprinkle with the sultanas/golden raisins.

Pour in the custard, grate a little nutmeg over the top, then sprinkle with the remaining sugar. Bake in the preheated oven for 18–20 minutes until firm. Leave to cool a little, then serve warm.

Traditional English bread and butter pudding, made with creamy custard and plump raisins, is delicious (see page 199). Arguably, it's even better made with rich Italian panettone and juicy blush plums.

panettone bread & butter pudding with plums

6 slices of panettone or other sweet bread, spread with butter

6 ripe plums, halved, pitted and sliced

300 ml/1¼ cups milk

100 ml/½ cup double/heavy cream

50 g/¼ cup unrefined caster/superfine sugar

3 eggs

a baking dish, ideally enamel, well buttered

serves 4

Cut the slices of buttered panettone in half and put a few slices of plum on top. Arrange in an overlapping layer in the prepared baking dish.

Put the milk, cream, sugar and eggs into a bowl and whisk. Pour the mixture over the panettone and plums. Chop any remaining plum slices into small pieces and sprinkle over the top. Set aside for 1 hour to let the panettone soak up the creamy liquid.

Preheat the oven to 180°C (350°F) Gas 4.

Cook in the preheated oven for about 35 minutes. Serve warm.

One of hundreds of versions of this classic, this one blanches the rice first to remove much of the starch, making it light and delicate. Traditional additions include fruit purées and chocolate or custard sauce.

rice pudding

125 g/½ cup risotto rice, such as arborio

500 ml/2 cups whole milk, boiled

60 g/⅓ cup sugar

1 vanilla pod/bean, split lengthways with a small sharp knife

15 g/1 tablespoon unsalted butter

a pinch of salt

a heatproof and ovenproof casserole or lidded baking dish

serves 4

Preheat the oven to 180°C (350°F) Gas 4.

Put the rice in a saucepan with a lid and add cold water to cover. Slowly bring to the boil over medium heat, then boil for 5 minutes. Drain the rice and rinse under cold water. Set aside to drain well.

Meanwhile, put the milk in a casserole dish with a lid and bring to the boil. Add the sugar and vanilla pod/bean. Remove from the heat, cover and leave to stand for 15 minutes. Using the tip of the knife, scrape out the vanilla seeds and stir them through the milk.

Add the rice to the milk, then add the butter and salt. Bring slowly to the boil. Cover and transfer to the preheated oven. Do not stir. Cook until the rice is tender and the liquid is almost completely absorbed but not dry, about 25–35 minutes. Serve warm.

Choose your favourite berries or stone fruit for this orange sponge pudding (but not strawberries). Vary according to the seasons; blueberries and blackberries make a particularly attractive deep purple pudding.

blueberry & cherry sponge pudding

500 g/1 lb. mixed fresh fruit such as pitted cherries and blueberries

125 g/½ cup caster/superfine sugar, plus 3 tablespoons extra

125 g/1 cup self-raising/rising flour

a pinch of salt

1 teaspoon baking powder

125 g/1¼ sticks unsalted butter, softened

2 large eggs, lightly beaten

finely grated zest of 1 orange

hot vanilla custard or cream, to serve

a 1.2-litre/5-cup pudding/ceramic bowl, greased and dredged with a little plain/all-purpose flour and caster/superfine sugar

serves 6–8

Preheat the oven to 180°C (350°F) Gas 4.

Reserve 125 g/½ cup of the fruit and 1 tablespoon of the sugar. Mix the remaining fruit with 2 tablespoons of the sugar, then transfer to the prepared pudding bowl.

Sift the flour, salt and baking powder into a second bowl. Put the softened butter and remaining 125 g/½ cup caster/superfine sugar into a mixing bowl and beat until very light, fluffy and creamy in colour. Add the eggs, a little at a time, beating between each addition, until the mixture is light and fluffy. Add the orange zest. Sift the flour mixture over the butter mixture, lightly fold in with a metal spoon, taking care not to over-mix: the mixture should drop softly off the spoon. If it is too stiff, fold in about 1 tablespoon water. Spoon the sponge mixture over the fruit, starting at the edges and working towards the centre. Smooth the top, making a slight indentation with the spoon in the middle so the mixture will rise evenly.

Bake in the preheated oven for 30–35 minutes until golden, well risen and as firm in the middle as it is at the sides. Remove from the oven and leave to settle a little before turning out onto a serving dish.

To make the sauce, blend the reserved fruit and sugar to a smooth purée. Serve the pudding with sauce and cream or custard.

Fresh berries are so good that it's tempting not to fuss with them too much, but they are very good used in a crumble. When serving blackberries or any red berry, add a splash of rosewater or orange blossom extract.

blackberry crumble

375 g/12 oz. blackberries (about 2 punnets/baskets)

1 tablespoon caster/superfine sugar

1 teaspoon cornflour/cornstarch

130 g/1 cup plain/all-purpose flour

75 g/5 tablespoons unsalted butter, chilled and cubed

60 g/¼ cup packed soft/light brown sugar

double/heavy cream, to serve

a baking dish, well buttered

serves 4

Put the blackberries in a bowl with the caster/superfine sugar and the cornflour/cornstarch and toss to mix. Tumble the berries into the prepared baking dish and set aside for 15–20 minutes.

Preheat the oven to 180°C (350°F) Gas 4.

Put the flour and butter in a large bowl and, using the tips of your fingers, rub the butter into the flour until the mixture resembles coarse breadcrumbs. Stir in the brown sugar.

Sprinkle the mixture evenly over the berries and bake in the preheated oven for 45–50 minutes until the top is golden brown.

Leave the crumble to cool slightly before serving with dollops of double/heavy cream spooned on top.

Pine nuts and almonds with their toasty flavours add another dimension to this crumble. The soft brown sugar thickens the plum juices to create a burgundy caramel which bubbles up to stain the nutty crust.

nutty plum crumble

12 plums, halved and pitted

2–3 thick strips of zest and the juice from 1 unwaxed orange

75 g/¹⁄₃ cup packed soft brown sugar

125 g/1 stick unsalted butter, chilled and cubed

100 g/¾ cup self-raising/rising flour

50 g/¹⁄₃ cup ground almonds

25 g/3 tablespoons flaked/slivered almonds

25 g/3 tablespoons pine nuts

pouring/light cream, to serve

a baking dish, well buttered

serves 4

Preheat the oven to 180°C (350°F) Gas 4.

Put the plums in the prepared baking dish. Add the orange zest and juice. Sprinkle over 2 tablespoons of the sugar and dot over about 2 tablespoons of the butter. Cover with foil and bake for 25–30 minutes, or until the plums are beginning to soften.

Put the flour, ground almonds and the remaining butter in a bowl (or a food processor) and rub (or pulse) until it forms lumps. Rub in the flaked/slivered almonds, pine nuts and the remaining sugar.

Remove the baking dish from the oven, discard the foil and scatter over the crumble topping. Bake for 30 minutes, or until the topping is golden and the juices are bubbling through. Remove from the oven and leave to stand for 10 minutes to allow the crust to firm up. Transfer to bowls and serve with cream.

If fresh or frozen cranberries are hard to find, buy dried ones and soak them for at least an hour in gently warmed cranberry juice before using. You can try making other topping shapes with cookie cutters.

cranberry & apple cobbler

450 g/1 lb. fresh or frozen cranberries or 200 g/7 oz. dried cranberries

450 g/1 lb. cooking apples

finely grated zest and juice of 1 small orange

150 g/¾ cup sugar

pinch of ground cloves

thick/heavy cream, to serve

cobbler topping

50 g/½ stick unsalted butter, chilled

225 g/1¾ cups self-raising/rising flour

a pinch of salt

50 g/¼ cup caster/superfine sugar

about 150 ml/⅔ cup milk, plus extra to glaze

a baking dish, well buttered

a 4–5-cm/1½–2-inch pastry/cookie cutter

serves 4

Pick over the cranberries and wash them. Peel and core the apples, then slice them thickly. Put 375 g/13 oz. of the cranberries and all the apples into a saucepan with the orange zest and juice, sugar and the cloves. Poach gently for 15–20 minutes until the fruit is juicy and tender. Set aside to cool and roughly chop the remaining cranberries.

Preheat the oven to 220°C (425°F) Gas 7.

Rub the butter into the flour and salt until it resembles fine breadcrumbs. Stir in the sugar and chopped cranberries. Add the milk to the flour, mixing with a blunt knife to form a fairly soft, sticky dough. Tip out onto a lightly floured work surface and roll out until 2 cm/¾ inch or slightly thicker. Cut out rounds using a fluted 4–5-cm/2-inch pastry cutter.

Spoon the fruit into the prepared baking dish and arrange the pastry rounds against the edge of the dish, overlapping them slightly and leaving a gap in the centre. Brush the top of the pastry rounds with milk. Bake in the preheated oven for 10–15 minutes, until the pastry is golden brown.

Remove from the oven and serve hot with thick/heavy cream.

The sugar in this decadent pudding melts into the cream around the bananas, making a rich and sticky sauce. Cutting the scone topping into little rounds helps it to cook faster and looks very decorative.

muscovado banana cobbler

4 medium bananas

150 ml/⅔ cup double/heavy cream or evaporated milk

2 tablespoons light muscovado/ light brown sugar

treacle scone topping

225 g/1¾ cups self-raising/rising flour

a pinch of salt

55 g/4 tablespoons unsalted butter

25 g/2 tablespoons caster/ superfine sugar

½ teaspoon ground cinnamon

3 tablespoons black treacle

150 ml/⅔ cup milk, plus extra to brush

pouring/light cream or vanilla ice cream, to serve

a baking dish

serves 4

Preheat the oven to 220°C (425°F) Gas 7.

Peel the bananas and slice thickly. Put them in a baking dish. Mix the cream or evaporated milk with the sugar and pour over the bananas.

To make the topping, sift the flour and salt into a bowl and rub in the butter. Mix in the sugar and cinnamon. Dissolve the treacle in the milk and quickly mix with the flour to form a soft dough. Knead this briefly on a floured work surface until smooth. Pat out to a thickness of 2 cm/ ¾ inch, no more, and cut into as many 3-cm/1-inch circles as you can, re-rolling the trimmings as necessary. Use these to cover the bananas.

Brush all over with a little milk and bake in the preheated oven for 15–20 minutes until well risen and golden brown on top. Cover with foil if the scones are cooking too quickly and the banana is still raw.

Serve warm with cream or vanilla ice cream.

These indulgent and chocolatey individual sponges are self-saucing. The option of a topping makes them very popular with chocoholics! Serve straight from the oven as the sponge quickly absorbs the sauce.

warm chocolate puddings

chocolate sauce

30 g/½ cup good-quality unsweetened cocoa powder

175 g/2½ cups packed soft brown sugar

chocolate puddings

125 g/1 cup plain/all-purpose flour

a pinch of salt

2 teaspoons baking powder

40 g/⅓ cup good-quality unsweetened cocoa powder

250 ml/1 cup whole milk

75 g/5 tablespoons unsalted butter, melted

125 g/½ cup plus 1 tablespoon caster/superfine sugar

2 eggs

1 teaspoon vanilla extract

crème fraîche, sour cream, mascarpone cheese or vanilla ice cream, to serve

hazelnut topping (optional)

100 ml/6 tablespoons pouring/ light cream

2 tablespoons soft brown sugar

50 g/2 oz. good-quality dark/ bittersweet chocolate

100 g/½ cup chocolate-hazelnut spread, such as Nutella

4 x 150-ml/5-oz ramekins

serves 4

Preheat the oven to 180°C (350°F) Gas 4.

First, make the chocolate sauce. Pour 200 ml/1 cup boiling water into a small saucepan, add the cocoa powder and brown sugar and lightly whisk over low heat making sure there are no lumps and the sugar has dissolved.

To make the puddings, sift the flour with the salt, baking powder and cocoa powder into a large bowl. Whisk in the milk, melted butter, caster/ superfine sugar, eggs and vanilla extract until a thick, smooth batter forms. Transfer the batter to a jug/pitcher, then pour it into the ramekins so that the mixture comes halfway up the sides. Place the ramekins on a baking sheet. Pour the chocolate sauce mixture carefully over the prepared puddings and bake in the preheated oven for 15–20 minutes; they should still be wobbly in the centre when they are ready.

While the puddings are cooking, make the hazelnut topping (if using). Put the cream and brown sugar in a small saucepan and bring to the boil, then remove from the heat. Finely chop the chocolate, add and stir until melted. Add the chocolate-hazelnut spread and stir until smooth.

Top each pudding with a dollop of crème fraîche, marscarpone or a scoop of vanilla ice cream and offer the hazelnut topping in a warm jug/ pitcher for pouring (if using).

Really, this is bread and butter pudding, using aged croissants. Chocolate croissants, brioche and even panettone will do. Embellish the recipe with chocolate chips, rum-soaked raisins or spoons of fruit conserve.

croissant pudding

4 all-butter croissants, preferably stale (but not too stale)

3 large eggs

300 ml/1¼ cups whole milk

3 heaped tablespoons crème fraîche, sour cream or double/heavy cream

50 g/¼ cup sugar, plus extra for sprinkling

a baking dish, well buttered

serves 4

Preheat the oven to 180°C (350°F) Gas 4.

Cut each croissant into 3 and arrange the pieces in the prepared baking dish. Put the eggs in a mixing bowl and beat well.

Put the milk, crème fraîche and sugar in a measuring jug/pitcher and whisk well. Pour into the beaten eggs and whisk again, then pour the mixture over the croissants. Sprinkle the top of the pudding liberally with sugar.

Bake in the preheated oven for 30–40 minutes until golden and the batter is just set. Serve warm.

Even the name of this pudding sounds nostalgic. This is a wonderfully indulgent ice cream sundae, based on an American classic — and is arguably even more amazing than the original.

knickerbocker glory

2 tablespoons chocolate sauce

4 scoops of vanilla ice cream

about 6–8 tablespoons fresh raspberries, crushed with a fork

2 scoops of strawberry ice cream

2–4 tablespoons chopped fresh fruit, such as pineapple or apricots

2–4 tablespoons whipped cream

about 2 teaspoons toasted flaked/ slivered almonds, coarsely crushed

2 glacé cherries

2 sundae or soda glasses and 2 long-handled parfait spoons

serves 2

Carefully spoon the chocolate sauce into the bottom of the glasses.

Add 1 scoop of vanilla ice cream, then about 1 tablespoon of the crushed fresh raspberries to each glass. Add 1 scoop of strawberry ice cream, then a layer of chopped fresh pineapple or apricots to each glass.

Add another scoop of vanilla ice cream and another layer of crushed raspberries. Top each one with a big cloud of whipped cream and sprinkle with toasted almonds.

Garnish with a glacé cherry, add a parfait spoon to each glass and serve immediately.

In this magnificent ice cream creation, hot fudge sauce contrasts with chilly ice cream and bananas. If that wasn't enough, whipped cream, toasted nuts and a cherry top everything off for a sinful splurge.

banana splits with hot fudge sauce

4 small bananas

4 scoops each of strawberry, vanilla and chocolate ice cream

4 maraschino cherries

60 g/½ cup pecan nuts, chopped and toasted

hot fudge sauce

90 g/3 oz. plain/semi-sweet chocolate, chopped

175 ml/¾ cup double/heavy cream

2 tablespoons butter

75 ml/¼ cup golden/light corn syrup

1 teaspoon vanilla extract

100 g/½ cup caster/superfine sugar

whipped vanilla cream

250 ml/1 cup double/heavy cream

1 tablespoon caster/superfine sugar

1 teaspoon vanilla extract

4 shallow, glass sundae dishes

serves 4

To make the hot fudge sauce, put the chocolate, cream and butter in a medium saucepan. When melted, add the syrup, vanilla extract and the sugar, stirring constantly over medium heat. When nearly boiling, turn the heat down to low and simmer for 15 minutes without stirring. Leave to cool for 5 minutes before using.

To make the whipped vanilla cream, whisk the double/heavy cream with the sugar and vanilla and set aside. Peel the bananas and cut in half lengthways.

Take the dishes and along the sides of each one, put 2 banana halves. Put one scoop of each flavour of ice cream between the bananas. Top with one spoonful of the whipped cream, a sprinkling of pecan nuts and a cherry on top. Serve with a small jug/pitcher of the hot fudge sauce to pour over the top.

Hot sauces make a delicious contrast with cold ice cream. The one featured here is butterscotch, but another scrumptious version to try is the hot fudge sauce on page 220.

hot butterscotch sundae

6 scoops of chocolate or vanilla ice cream

2 scoops of coffee or vanilla ice cream

ready-made nut brittle, crushed into small pieces or toasted nuts

hot butterscotch sauce

100 g/½ cup soft brown sugar

130 ml/½ cup double/heavy cream

5 tablespoons butter

2 metal or glass heatproof ice cream bowls

serves 2

To make the hot butterscotch sauce, put all the ingredients in a saucepan and stir over medium heat until melted and boiling. Reduce the heat and simmer for 3 minutes. Serve hot as the sauce will set when cold. Any leftover sauce can be kept, covered, in the fridge and used another time.

Put 3 scoops of chocolate or vanilla ice cream in the base of each bowl and balance 1 scoop of coffee or vanilla ice cream on top.

Spoon about 2–3 tablespoons hot butterscotch sauce into each bowl, scatter with pieces of nut brittle or toasted nuts and serve immediately.

This recipe is the real thing — a dense, rich cheesecake with a crunchy base. Enjoy a slice with your favourite cup of coffee and imagine that you and your friends are in a New York deli!

traditional new york cheesecake

base

200 g/8 oz. digestive biscuits/graham crackers

100 g/1 stick unsalted butter

75 g/¼ cup plus 2 tablespoons caster/superfine sugar

filling

150 g/1½ sticks unsalted butter

170 g/¾ cup caster/superfine sugar

4 large eggs, beaten

30 g/3 tablespoons plain/all-purpose flour

finely grated zest and juice of 1 large unwaxed lemon

½ teaspoon vanilla extract

675 g/3 x 8 oz. packages full-fat soft cheese

60 ml/¼ cup milk

topping

425 ml/1¾ cups sour cream

1 tablespoon icing/confectioners' sugar

freshly squeezed juice of 1 lemon

a springform cake pan, 23-cm/9-inch diameter, greased

serves 10–12

To make the base, preheat the oven to 190°C (375°F) Gas 5. Put the biscuits/crackers in a food processor and process until finely crumbed. Gently melt the butter in a small saucepan, then stir in the crumbs and sugar. Spread the crumb mixture over the base of the prepared pan, pressing down lightly. Stand the pan on a baking sheet and cook in the preheated oven for 8–10 minutes. Remove from the oven and leave to cool.

Reduce the temperature to 160°C (325°F) Gas 3. To make the filling, put the butter and sugar in a large bowl and, using a wooden spoon or electric hand mixer, beat until pale and fluffy. Gradually beat in the eggs. Mix in the flour, lemon zest, lemon juice and vanilla extract. Put the soft cheese in a separate bowl and beat until smooth. Gently beat in the milk, then gradually beat in the butter and sugar mixture. Spoon the mixture over the base and level the surface. Bake in the preheated oven for 1½ hours.

Meanwhile, make the topping. Put the sour cream, icing/confectioners' sugar and lemon juice in a large bowl and, using a wooden spoon or electric hand mixer, beat lightly. Chill in the refrigerator until required.

Remove the cheesecake from the oven and increase the temperature to 190°C (375°F) Gas 5. Pour the topping over the cheesecake, level and return to the oven for a further 10 minutes or until set. Turn off the oven, leave the door ajar and let the cheesecake cool in the oven to prevent it cracking. Alternatively, transfer it to a wire rack, invert a large bowl over the cake, then let cool. Chill the cheesecake for 2 hours before serving.

This creamy cheesecake holds rivulets of raspberry and chocolate sauces in a crisp chocolate biscuit case. If your time is limited, fold fresh raspberries and grated chocolate into the cheese mixture instead of the sauces.

raspberry & chocolate ripple cheesecake

base

100 g/1 stick butter

2 tablespoons soft brown sugar

250 g/8 oz. plain chocolate digestive biscuits/graham crackers, finely crushed

filling

350 g/1½ x 8 oz. packages full-fat soft cheese

3 eggs, separated

100 g/½ cup caster/superfine sugar

1 teaspoon vanilla extract

200 ml/1 cup double/heavy cream

20 g/3 envelopes powdered gelatine

chocolate and raspberry ripple

250 g/8 oz. fresh or frozen raspberries

50 g/¼ cup caster/superfine sugar

50 g/2 oz. plain/semi-sweet chocolate

2 tablespoons double/heavy cream

a loose-based, 20-cm/8-inch diameter cake pan, greased and lined

serves 8

For the base, gently melt the butter and sugar in a saucepan, then stir in the biscuit/cracker crumbs. Press the crumb mixture evenly over the base and up the sides of the pan. Chill for at least 30 minutes.

To make the filling, beat the soft cheese until softened. Beat in the egg yolks and half the caster/superfine sugar, vanilla extract and cream. Dissolve the gelatine in 2 tablespoons of water in a small heatproof bowl, set over a saucepan of hot water and stir occasionally. Keep it warm.

Make the raspberry ripple: put the raspberries and sugar in a saucepan, heat gently until the sugar dissolves, then boil for 1 minute until slightly thickened. Press through a sieve/strainer and leave to cool. To make the chocolate ripple, melt the chocolate and cream in another saucepan, then stir well and leave to cool until just warm, but still pourable.

Beat the gelatine into the cheese mixture. Put the egg whites in a clean bowl, whisk until stiff but not dry, then whisk in the remaining sugar, spoonful by spoonful, until thick after each addition. Beat 2 spoonfuls of the meringue into the cheese mixture, then quickly fold in the rest. Spoon dollops of mixture over the base so they join up, then pour the raspberry and chocolate sauces in between the mixture. Spoon in the remaining cheese mixture and pour again (keep any remaining sauces to serve). Swirl the mixtures together with a skewer to produce a ripple effect. Give the pan a shake, then chill for about 2–4 hours until set.

Ground ginger and molasses are the keys to any successful gingerbread recipe. Grated fresh ginger or chopped stem ginger can be used to add a little texture if you wish.

gingerbread pancakes

285 g/1½ cups plain/all-purpose flour

2 teaspoons baking powder

½ teaspoon bicarbonate of/ baking soda

½ teaspoon salt

2 teaspoons ground ginger

2 teaspoons ground cinnamon

1 teaspoon ground cloves

2 eggs

55 g/¼ cup firmly packed light brown sugar

250 ml/1 cup buttermilk

2 tablespoons molasses

4 tablespoons unsalted butter, melted and cooled

apple marmalade and crème fraîche/sour cream, to serve

a cast-iron griddle/grill pan (optional)

makes 12 pancakes

Sift the flour, baking powder, bicarbonate of/baking soda, salt, ginger, cinnamon and cloves into a bowl. Put the eggs and brown sugar into a second bowl and whisk well with a wire whisk. Whisk in the buttermilk, molasses, cooled melted butter and 125 ml/½ cup water. Add the flour mixture and whisk once or twice until almost smooth. Do not overwork the mixture – remember lumps are good.

Lightly grease and preheat a griddle or heavy frying pan/skillet over medium heat. Reduce the heat. Pour about 2 tablespoons of batter into the pan, spread with the back of a spoon and cook in batches of 3–4 for 1 minute over low heat, until small bubbles begin to appear on the surface and the underside is golden brown. Turn them over and cook the other side for 1 minute. Transfer to a plate and keep them warm in a low oven while you cook the remainder.

Serve with apple marmalade and cool crème fraîche/sour cream.

Attention: calling all chocoholics for a complete overload! Packed with velvety melted chocolate and finished with the sweet and sour taste of smooth white chocolate yoghurt. Perfection.

triple chocolate pancakes

285 g/1½ cups plain/all-purpose flour

75 g/¾ cup unsweetened cocoa powder

1 teaspoon baking powder

1 teaspoon bicarbonate of/ baking soda

55 g/¼ cup caster/superfine sugar

200 ml/¾ cup milk

125 ml/½ cup buttermilk

2 eggs, separated

30 g/3 tablespoons unsalted butter, melted and cooled

½ teaspoon salt

100 g/3 oz. dark/bittersweet chocolate, chopped

100 g/3 oz. white chocolate, chopped

good-quality chocolate sauce, warmed, to serve

white chocolate yoghurt

150 g/6 oz. white chocolate

4 tablespoons Greek yoghurt

a cast-iron griddle pan (optional)

makes about 12 pancakes

Sift the flour, cocoa, baking powder, bicarbonate of/baking soda and sugar into a bowl. Put the milk, buttermilk, egg yolks and cooled melted butter into a second large bowl and beat well. Add the flour mixture and mix thoroughly.

Put the egg whites and salt into a grease-free bowl and whisk until stiff peaks form. Add 1 tablespoon of the egg whites to the chocolate mixture and stir to loosen it, then carefully fold in the remaining egg whites, then the dark and white chocolate.

Lightly grease a griddle pan or heavy frying pan/skillet and preheat over medium heat. Reduce the heat. Pour about 2 tablespoons of batter into the pan and cook in batches of 3–4 over low heat for about 1 minute, or until small bubbles begin to appear on the surface and the underside is golden brown. Turn the pancakes over and cook the other side for 1 minute. Transfer to a plate and keep them warm in a low oven while you cook the remainder.

To make the white chocolate yoghurt, put the chocolate into a bowl set over a saucepan of simmering water and melt slowly. Remove from the heat and leave to cool a little, then beat in the yoghurt until smooth and shiny. Serve with the pancakes and warmed chocolate sauce.

A classic brunch dish with a twist! If you don't have a waffle iron, you can still enjoy the flavour: simply drop a ladle of batter onto a lightly greased, heated frying pan/skillet and fry until golden on both sides.

waffles with maple syrup ice cream

maple syrup ice cream

500 ml/2 cups double/heavy cream

250 ml/1 cup milk

seeds from 1 vanilla pod/bean

5 egg yolks

125 ml/½ cup maple syrup, plus extra to serve

waffles

150 g/1 cup plus 2 tablespoons plain/all-purpose flour

1 teaspoon baking powder

½ teaspoon bicarbonate of/ baking soda

1 tablespoon caster/superfine sugar

125 ml/½ cup buttermilk

1 egg, lightly beaten

75 g/5 tablespoons butter, melted

a waffle iron (optional)

serves 6

To make the ice cream, put the cream, milk and vanilla seeds into a saucepan and heat until the mixture reaches boiling point. Remove from the heat and set aside.

Meanwhile, put the egg yolks and syrup in a bowl and beat. Stir in the heated cream mixture and return to the pan. Heat gently, stirring, until the mixture thickens enough to coat the back of a wooden spoon. Do not boil or the mixture will curdle. Remove from the heat and leave to cool. Freeze in an ice cream maker, following the manufacturer's instructions. If you don't have an ice cream maker, pour the mixture into flat freezer trays and put them in the freezer. Leave the mixture to partially freeze, beat to break up the ice crystals and return the trays to the freezer. Repeat several times – the more you do it, the smoother the end result.

To make the waffles, lightly grease and preheat a waffle iron. Sift the flour, baking powder and bicarbonate of/baking soda into a bowl. Stir in the sugar. Beat the remaining ingredients together in a second bowl, then beat into the dry ingredients until smooth.

Spoon a layer of the batter into the heated waffle iron and spread flat. Cook for about 1 minute until crisp and golden. Serve hot with a scoop of ice cream and a little extra maple syrup.

For the best pastry, freeze the butter and shortening before making the dough and use a glass or metal pie plate. When making, be sure to get the flour and butters to the crumb stage before mixing in the water.

basic pie case

150 g/1 cup plus 2 tablespoons plain/all-purpose flour

a pinch of salt

90 g/6 tablespoons unsalted butter, frozen

30 g/2 tablespoons pure vegetable shortening, frozen

1 egg white, to seal

a glass or metal pie plate, 23-cm/9-inch diameter

makes sufficient pastry for a 23-cm/9-inch pastry case

Combine the flour and salt in a large bowl. Chop the butter and shortening into 2-cm/1-inch pieces and add to the bowl. Using a pastry blender or two knives, chop through the mixture until it resembles coarse breadcrumbs. Add 3 tablespoons iced water and bring the mixture together with a fork. Add additional water if necessary until it comes together with your hands. Very quickly knead the dough into a ball. Don't handle it for too long or it will become warm. Flatten the dough into a disc, cover in clingfilm/plastic wrap and refrigerate for 1 hour.

To roll the dough, work on a large surface that is not near a warm stove or dishwasher. Sprinkle flour over the area and a rolling pin. Dust both sides of the dough with flour and roll out. When it is 30 cm/12 inches in diameter, gently and loosely wrap the dough around the rolling pin. Unwrap the dough over the pie plate and press it into the bottom and sides. Trim the edges leaving a 3-cm/1¼-inch overhang. Turn the edges under and press to form a crust. Use your fingers to crimp it all around the edge of the dish. Place in the freezer for at least 30 minutes.

To bake the pie case blind, preheat the oven to 200°C (400°F) Gas 6. Cover the chilled pastry with a large sheet of wax paper. Fill with baking beans and bake for 15 minutes. Remove the paper and beans, brush the case with the egg white and bake for a further 8 minutes. Remove and leave to cool on a rack.

This wonderfully light and crumbly pastry is enriched with egg and made with butter only. Use it for richer pies and tarts, or where the pastry is more than just a carrier for the filling and its taste is important.

sweet shortcrust pastry

250 g/1¾ cups plain/all-purpose flour

2 tablespoons icing/confectioners' sugar

½ teaspoon salt

125 g/1 stick unsalted butter, chilled and cubed

2 egg yolks

2 tablespoons iced water

a metal tart or flan pan, 23-cm/9-inch diameter

makes sufficient pastry for a 23-cm/9-inch sweet pastry case

Sift the flour, icing/confectioners' sugar and salt together into a bowl, then rub in the butter. Mix the egg yolks with the 2 tablespoons iced water. Add to the flour, mixing together lightly with a knife. The pastry must have some water in it or it will be too difficult to handle. If it is still too dry, add a little more water, sprinkling it over the flour mixture 1 tablespoon at a time.

Turn the mixture out onto a lightly floured work surface. Knead lightly with your hands until smooth. Form the dough into a rough ball. Flatten slightly, then wrap in clingfilm/plastic wrap and chill for at least 30 minutes before rolling out. Roll out and bake blind following the instructions given on page 192.

Note The pastry can be made in a food processor, which is quicker and easier, and there is no sticky mess to clear up. But the classic method described here gives a slightly lighter result.

index

recipe credits

Fiona Beckett
Boeuf bourguignon
Pot roast brisket with
   Zinfandel
Pumpkin soup with
   honey and sage
Smoked salmon
   kedgeree
Sticky toffee pudding
   cake

Susannah Blake
Banoffee cupcakes
Gooey chocolate and
   hazelnut cupcakes
Melting cheese and
   sun-dried tomatoes
   on toast
Mushrooms on toast
Rocky road cupcakes
Spicy fried potatoes
   and chorizo on toast
Sticky fried bananas on
   toast
Tuna melt

Tessa Bramley
Blueberry and cherry
   sponge pudding

Maxine Clark
A big pot of cassoulet
Cranberry and apple
   cobbler
Green lasagne with
   ricotta, pesto and
   mushrooms
Muscovado banana
   cobbler
Perfect mashed
   potatoes
Polenta baked with
   Italian sausage and
   cheese
Pork loin roasted with
   rosemary and garlic
Raspberry and
   chocolate ripple
   cheesecake
Sweet shortcrust
   pastry
Traditional New York
   cheesecake
Walnut tart with quick
   fudge ice cream

Linda Collister
Best-ever chocolate
   cake
Brownie fudge pie
Butterscotch blondies
Choc fudge cookies
Classic choc chip
   cookies
Cornmeal and bacon
   muffins
Extra-crunchy peanut
   butter cookies
Fudgy yet flourless
   brownies
Toad-in-the-hole
Maple syrup pecan
   cake

Ross Dobson
Baked ziti pasta with
   aubergine, basil and
   ricotta
Blackberry crumble
Chicken, leek and
   tarragon pot pie
Creamy cauliflower and
   Gruyère soup
Dusky apple pie
Egg, bacon and spinach
   pie
Pumpkin and
   gorgonzola risotto
Roast beef with winter
   vegetables and garlic
   crème
Roasted pork with
   apple and fennel
   puddings
Sage pork chops with
   colcannon mash
Sausages with winter
   rosti
Scotch broth
Smashed roast
   potatoes
Smoky sausage and
   bean casserole
Strawberry buttermilk
   cake

Ursula Ferrigno
Four cheeses risotto
Mushrooms, Cognac
   and cream risotto

Silvana Franco
Basic pizza dough
Chicago deep pan
   pepperoni pizza
Fiorentina pizza
Roasted pepper pizza

Tonia George
Beef polpetti with
   tomato sauce and
   spaghetti
Chunky puy lentil and
   vegetable soup
Nutty plum crumble

Kate Habershon
Gingerbread pancakes
Triple chocolate
   pancakes

Rachael Anne Hill
Baked sweet potatoes
   with cheesy lentil
   hash and bacon
Fish cakes
Fish pie

Jennifer Joyce
Bacon, potato, red
   Leicester panini with
   Tabasco panini
Banana splits with hot
   fudge sauce
Basic pie case
Chicken noodle soup
Chocolate-hazelnut
   banana brioche
Corned beef hash
Huevos rancheros
Lemon meringue pie
Wicked macaroni
   cheese
Toasted ham and
   cheese sandwiches

Caroline Marson
Roasted vegetable
   soup
Warm chocolate
   puddings

Jane Noraika
Butternut squash and
   goats' cheese gratin

**Elsa Petersen-
Schepelern**
Hot butterscotch
   sundae
Knickerbocker glory

Louise Pickford
BLT tortilla panini
Bread and butter
   pudding
Classic all-American
   hamburger
Eggs benedict
Home-made baked
   beans in tomato
   sauce
Panettone French toast
Pan-fried chicken with
   creamy beans and
   leeks
Steak sandwich
Waffles with maple
   syrup ice cream

Jennie Shapter
Baked brunch omelette

Sonia Stevenson
Lancashire hotpot
Pot roast with braised
   root vegetables
Tuscan pork and bean
   casserole

Fran Warde
Carrot cake
Courgettes and
   cheddar on toast
Daube of beef
French toast and fried
   tomatoes
Panettone bread and
   butter pudding
Scrambled eggs
Seafood lasagne
Shepherd's pie
Steak and mushroom
   pie

Laura Washburn
Cauliflower gratin
Chicken sauté with
   carrots, leeks,
   mustard and cream
Chili with all the
   trimmings
Chocolate chip cake
Creamy potato gratin
Croissant pudding
French onion soup
Rice pudding
Sticky spareribs with
   orange-chilli glaze

photography credits

Key: a=above, b=below, r=right, l=left, c=centre.

Martin Brigdale
Pages 3r, 4, 6br, 8-9
background, 10, 13,
42, 50, 53, 56-57
background, 70, 94,
97, 98-99 background,
143, 148, 151, 152-153
backgrounds, 162,
165, 166, 188-189
background, 194, 197,
202, 221, 225,226, 234,
240

Richard Jung
Pages 3l, 3cl, 3cr, 6al, 7,
17, 18, 56c, 65, 66, 86,
93, 98l, 98c, 100, 103,
111, 113, 132, 147, 152c,
154, 178, 180, 188c,
190, 193, 206, 209

Peter Cassidy
Pages 14, 22, 41, 62,
85, 116, 119, 120, 135,
136, 169, 188l, 198,
210, 213, 214

William Lingwood
Pages 2, 8l, 8r, 25, 26,
29, 30, 56l, 56r, 73, 74,
77, 78, 107, 123, 124,
139, 184, 229, 230

Debi Treloar
Pages 5, 6ar, 6bl, 37,
38, 98r, 104, 108, 140,
188r, 201, 218, 223

Diana Miller
Pages 152l, 152r, 158,
173, 174, 177

William Reavell
Pages 1, 8c, 21, 33, 69,
183

David Munns
Pages 115, 127, 131,
157, 217

Noel Murphy
Pages 81, 83, 90, 128,
144

Ian Wallace
Pages 34, 46, 187, 233

Caroline Arber
Pages 45, 161

Jason Lowe
Pages 58, 61

Vanessa Davies
Pages 89, 170

Tara Fisher
Page 49

Christine Hanscomb
Page 205

Philip Webb
Page 54